Thaddeus Barnum is an unusually gifted preacher, teacher, mentor, and author. Everything he has written has illuminated my mind and stirred my heart. I want to get his latest offering, *Real Identity*, into the hands of as many people as possible. It is rich food for the soul.

—LYLE W. DORSETT, Billy Graham professor of evangelism, Beeson Divinity School, Samford University; senior pastor, Christ the King Anglican Church, Birmingham, Alabama

It's so refreshing to hear someone ask the hard questions about God and life, which Thad so ably does while encouraging us with the news that the answers are out there.

—JULIA DUIN, former religion editor, *The Washington Times*; author of *Quitting Church* and *Days of Fire and Glory*

Thad Barnum challenges us to congruity between the outside and the inside, between what we seem to be and what we actually are, between the mind and the heart. He also shows us how it is the Bible that lights our paths, with God's Spirit making these connections in our lives. What happens when disciples are challenged by great adversity or hidden temptation? Do we walk the talk then? Or was it just talk? How the church might be strengthened by wide distribution of *Real Identity*!

—ROBERT DUNCAN, archbishop ⸍⸍⸍ ⸍⸍⸍ North America

As I read *Real Identity*, my eyes became moist with tears and my heart was moved toward longing for more of Christ. Every chapter left me wanting more, wanting to meet the people in the stories, wanting to walk more closely with the God of the story.

—NANCY GUTHRIE, author of Seeing Jesus
in the Old Testament Bible study series

In *Real Identity*, Thad Barnum lifts us out of what so often feels like a frustrating maze of discipleship. He demonstrates for us what is always needed to follow Jesus well: putting our actual lives as we now experience it on the table before God. When we do, lots of good things happen: the Bible comes alive, God's grace is seen for the unspeakable power it is, and we find gentle, consistent healing and change. I commend *Real Identity* to anyone seeking a fresh start in their relationship with Jesus.

—TODD HUNTER, bishop; author of *Christianity
Beyond Belief* and *Our Favorite Sins*

One of the most unique devotionals I have ever read—it is one that disciples the soul—Barnum clothes Scripture texts with the real lives of twenty-first-century people. Out of this lens comes the brilliance of Jesus in all His beauty and compelling ways. Each section calls for stopping and pondering. The result will be a new level of listening to God.

—JO ANNE LYON, General Superintendent, The Wesleyan Church

The distance between knowing *about* God and actually knowing God is infinite. In wonderfully readable prose, my friend Thad Barnum helps us see what it means to know God and live the real life He intended for us when He made us. It's actually possible, and since it's also the most important thing in the universe, I'm thrilled to recommend this book.

—ERIC METAXAS, *New York Times* best-selling author
of *Bonhoeffer: Pastor, Martyr, Prophet, Spy* and
7 Men and the Secret of Their Greatness

There is a great deal of healthful Christian reality in these pages.

—J. I. PACKER, Board of Governors' professor
of theology, Regent College; author; theologian

Barnum's stories walk us through the experiences of a wide variety of people in their relationships to God, especially as they experienced pain and struggle. Life encounters Scripture and leaves us somehow changed, somehow further along on the journey. Somewhere in these pages you will find yourself and see your own way forward in your walk with God.

—KENNETH SCHENCK, academic dean and
professor at Wesley Seminary in Marion, Indiana;
author of *God's Plan Fulfilled* and the Paul series (WPH)

Having known Thad and the congregation he leads for several years, I can attest that he lives what he preaches. He is a scholar who helps us with the practical application of timeless biblical truth. In the pulpit, he is a passionate communicator who connects with his audience. One thing I liked about *Real Identity* is that Thad writes with the same passion and practical application with which he preaches. He takes me to a better place and does so in a way that I can understand. *Real Identity* confronts my reality with Scripture and illustrations from the real lives of real people, like me!

—TERRY WILCOX, Wesleyan pastor;
executive director, Bridgeport Rescue Mission

REAL
IDENTITY

WHERE BIBLE AND LIFE MEET

THADDEUS BARNUM

wesleyan
publishing
house

Indianapolis, Indiana

Copyright © 2013 by Thaddeus Barnum
Published by Wesleyan Publishing House
Indianapolis, Indiana 46250
Printed in the United States of America
ISBN: 978-0-089827-755-5
ISBN (e-book): 978-0-89827-756-2

Library of Congress Cataloging-in-Publication Data

Barnum, Thaddeus.
  Real identity : where Bible and life meet / Thaddeus Barnum.
    pages cm
  Includes bibliographical references and index.
  ISBN 978-0-89827-755-5 (alk. paper)
  1. Bible. Gospels--Meditations. 2. Bible. Genesis--Meditations. I. Title.
  BS2555.54.B37 2013
  242'.5--dc23

                          2013031237

My wife, Erilynne, and I dedicate this book to our beloved dads. These are men who imprinted our lives with the gospel of our Lord Jesus Christ:
Eric Ludwig Forsberg, and
Malcolm "Mac" McGregor Barnum.
We are eternally grateful.

Other books by Thaddeus Barnum include:
Never Silent, *Remember Eve*, and
Where Is God in Suffering and Tragedy?

For more information about these and other
discipleship resources, visit the call2disciple ministry
website at www.call2disciple.com.

CONTENTS

PREFACE

In the fall of 1979, I sat at my typewriter—yes, typewriter—and transcribed dozens of Bible teachings my wife Erilynne had given. Her heart, her passion, was to lay down the first principles of Scripture in a way that discipled the soul. She believed—I believed—that Bible knowledge alone doesn't do that.

There has to be a way for Bible and life to meet.

Eventually, we married. Eventually, these teachings developed into a course of study that was filmed on DVD and used in small groups across the country (www.call2disciple.com). As the years passed, we still felt a burden weighing upon us. We saw too many people strong in Bible knowledge and active in church and ministry, but in times of testing—when real character is exposed—doing and saying what should never be done and said in the Christian family.

We need our souls discipled in Christ Jesus. If we are to be effective for the kingdom of God and our King, we need identity—real identity—that's found in Him working deep in us, transforming us. Way beyond outward appearance.

It's here where these devotions were born. Each one assumes you've studied the passage and your expositional work is done. Then it's time to ask the questions: "How do we connect with the text? How will the Holy Spirit take His Word and form it inside us for change, real change?"

This is our prayer: "Lord, conform us to the image of Your Son" (see Rom. 8:29).

This book follows Erilynne's first year of her discipleship course. Though I've done the writing, she's been the designer and architect. So let me say first: Erilynne, my love, thank you, well done! You amaze me. Always.

We both want to thank Jan Buchanan and Susan Wyskiel (our daughters) for their love and care in overseeing "call2disciple." Jan is my sounding board. Susan and, early on, our dear friend Nancy Bryan, took these devotions and made them come alive on our website. Incredible job, incredible women.

We are also indebted to Kate, Ken, David, Barbara, Lyle, and countless others who have rigorously prayed for us and this writing project. To our staff, parish council, and church family at Apostles in Fairfield, Connecticut, thank you for your constant encouragement. You bring life to us.

We are thrilled to be so graciously welcomed into the family of Wesleyan Publishing House. We are especially thankful for Rachael Stevenson, who ensured the quality of copyediting and proofing; Lyn Rayn, who designed the cover and interior; and Jeff Ray and Jaymie Shook, who launch this book to the world through marketing and sales.

But I must say a special thanks to Craig Bubeck, who acquired, edited, and directed the publication of this work. You are a dear friend and a gifted man. Your love for the Lord makes me love Him more—and write more. Thank you.

To God be the glory.

—THADDEUS R. BARNUM

INTRODUCTION

―――✒―――

MAKE ME REAL, LORD

I lead a Bible study at the local rescue mission with fifteen guys who've come off the streets. Every week they show me what it means to daily choose Jesus Christ. They say it a thousand times, "I can do all things through [Christ] who strengthens me" (Phil. 4:13). And they believe it. They won't do life without Him.

We open with prayer. We turn to the Bible, and I feel the challenge. They don't want just an academic study; they want connection. The crossings that connect the mind and heart. The truth of God's Word to my life and theirs. They need the gospel to be what the gospel really is, "the power of God for salvation" (Rom. 1:16).

They need more than true. They need practical. They need real.

A staff member comes in. He asks if anyone has seen Joe. They say he was at breakfast an hour ago but no one has seen him since. They're concerned for him. He'd been at the mission a few months and made great strides.

The men pray for Joe. They ask the Lord to help him. "If he's back on the streets, Lord," one of them prays, "help him make right decisions and keep him safe."

They finish their prayers, open their Bibles, and look at me like they don't want me to mess up. They need the truth of God's Word today. Truth they can understand. Truth that's real manna feeding their souls. Truth that comes in the strength and power of the Holy Spirit to live life today.

I have to make the connection. I have to be real so they can live real.

We start at the beginning. Back to Genesis. Back to when God created the heavens and earth in perfection. Back to when we were made in His image and created, not for corruption and evil, but for God and His glory. We deal with the entrance of sin, evil, and corruption. The reign of the Devil and death.

"If we're going to know Him, if we're going to serve Him," I tell the men, "we have to hear the whole story. He made us for good, and He wants good for us. We're the ones who sinned. We did that. Not Him. And in His kindness, He did something about it. It's why He sent His Son. He wants good for us."

Good is hard to hear when you've been lost in a world of bad.

They push me. They want to know how I know. They want stories—real stories—from when I first crossed over from my bad, my sin, my real sin, to when His good first touched my heart and soul. Not just my mind. Me.

And they push. They want to see my crossings.

I resist. I always resist because I hate exposing me. I'd rather keep things in the realm of concept. Thoughts. Principles. So I can protect my heart.

But they push because their lives aren't lived there. They need *His* good. They need it to grab their minds, hearts, and souls and give them the power they need to choose good today in Jesus' name. Real good. Real power. Filling their souls.

Especially today. Though no one knows for sure where Joe is, they all know where Joe is—he's back on the street. And they don't want that. Not for him. Not for them. Not today. The streets cannot have them today. They choose to stay together. They choose Jesus.

And so do I.

Sitting in that room, in a big circle, we are brothers in Christ. They suffer from years of drug enslavement. I don't. But I suffer, like them, from my slavery to sin and the power of that sin trying to control my life.

I choose Jesus today, like them. I need Jesus today, like them. I need to hear the Word of the Lord to my soul. And I need it to be "the power of God for salvation" that saved me once, that saves me now.

So we build and cross our paths together. Starting in Genesis, moving to Exodus. Pointing to the day when Jesus Christ comes and makes all things real. He's the One who deals with our sin, addictions, pride, and rebellion by what

He did on the cross. He's the One who makes it possible to live today.

We build as we go, crisscrossing paths, roads, and highways together—all of them, our crossroads, captured in the book you now hold, inviting you to go, inviting you to pray with us. Lord, take us to where Bible and life meet.

PART 1

REAL
IN JESUS

1

THE CROSSING

Reflections on Mark 4:1–20 and Matthew 7:24–27

*And the rain fell, and the floods came, and the winds
blew and slammed against that house; and yet it did
not fall, for it had been founded on the rock.*

—MATTHEW 7:25

Here I stand. At the crossing.

Sometimes I wish it wasn't so hard to find. That what
we see on the outside is what's real on the inside. Just that
simple. But too often the chasm between the two is huge.

And I forget about the crossing, where the outside and
inside meet.

Sam taught me that years ago. He was the perfect testimony.
He came to faith in Christ through the witness of Christian
men in our church. And Sam jumped in—Bible studies, home
group, ministries in the church and our local community.
He gave time, which in his profession he had little of. He
gave money to the church and beyond . . . way beyond.

Because he cared for the needy. It hurt him to see people
suffering. Off he went on mission trips to remote parts of
the world, wanting to help, needing to serve, having a big
heart.

His name came up to serve in church leadership. Who could be better? He met all the criteria: strong in belief, in conduct, in service, in leadership.

Sam.

Until the testing came, and it came hard. By the time we heard about it, it was too late. Sam had left his job, left his wife, left his teenage kids, left his church family. Sam was gone. The guys closest to him at church pursued him. They still do, even to this day so many years later.

Some said it was an affair. Others said something big happened at work. Was he caught doing drugs? Smuggling money? A cover-up of some kind? It almost doesn't matter. Whatever it was, it was big enough to expose his heart.

And that's what testing does.

In the parable of the sower, the seed of God's Word has to land in the heart—the good soil. If not, when testing comes, we fall away (Mark 4:17).

In the same way, the foundation has to be on rock, not sand. So when the storm comes, we stand strong, unshaken (Matt. 7:25).

Jesus taught us this. The world is full of trial and trouble. What matters is that we're ready for it—that what He has done in us is real. To the heart. And what He will do for us is see us through the storm. He will give us what we need to endure. To persevere.

That's His promise (John 16:33).

James said it. All we have to do is ask. In the midst of the mess of this world, we ask the Lord "who gives to all generously and without reproach," and He gives us the wisdom we need in the moment (James 1:5). As long as we ask in faith. And from faith.

Because our faith is real. He has penetrated our hearts.

But that's the problem, isn't it?

Sam looked so real. He said the right words. He did the right things. He leapt beyond himself for the sake of others. He wept at the reading of Scripture. He showed us what it means to have a passion for the things of God. He testified in- and outside church. He looked so real.

None of us dreamed that he lived in two worlds. One on the outside. One on the inside. And the one on the inside was so dark and secretive, controlled and well-protected, that none of us saw it coming. A big storm. Bigger than him. Exposing him. Tearing his two worlds apart.

Double-minded, that's what James called it (James 1:8). A word meaning "two-souled," it's deeper than being two-faced—hypocrites with an image on the outside that betrays the heart on the inside.

It goes to the breaking of the soul. As if, deep in our cores, we can be two.

And we can't. Not before God. Never, never can we serve two masters and get away with it (Matt. 6:24). No matter how in control we think we are.

Because storms come. Storms expose.

Sam became exactly what James said: "Like the surf of the sea, driven and tossed by the wind" (James 1:6). The storm hit and he was gone. His wife, teenage kids, and church family bereft without him. His kids ached for their dad. One of them wondered if being a Christian was really even worth it.

Sam.

He taught me to stand at the crossing.

He taught me that it's not enough, as a Christian leader, to help people believe in Jesus Christ, know the Bible, learn to pray, belong to the church, grow in service and ministry, give from our resources, and serve the poor, the needy, the voiceless.

All of it can be done and the heart never touched, the gospel never made real. The salvation given us in Jesus Christ never known in the depths of who we are. Outward Christians: right words, right deeds, playing games, two-souled.

So I make myself stand at the crossing.

Between the outside and the inside. And I beg the Lord to have mercy on us. To help us cross. So that Jesus Christ is real to our hearts, in the depths of our souls, before the storms come.

So we're not like Sam—disciples on the wrong foundation, rooted in the wrong soil, double-minded, two-souled, rudderless at the time of testing. But just the opposite. We know Him. He knows us.

We've made the crossing. We've found real.

QUESTIONS FOR REFLECTION*

Can you talk about what it's like to stand at the crossing between the image you project and who you really are?

Is Jesus Christ real for you? Is He the foundation on which your life is built?

---

* The reflection at the end of each devotion is designed to encourage prayer, journaling, and conversation in small group settings. It's easy to read and go on. It's better to read, stop, and engage in dialogue and prayer.

2

HELP ME STAY HERE

Reflections on Luke 9:18–27

*If anyone wishes to come after Me, he must deny himself,
and take up his cross daily and follow Me. For whoever wishes
to save his life will lose it, but whoever loses his life for
My sake, he is the one who will save it.*

—LUKE 9:23–24

It's hard to stay here—at the crossing.

Just like it's hard to be in battle, on the front lines, and suddenly find I have no shields. No lines of defense. Nothing to protect me, my heart, my soul.

And here I stand. Exposed. Vulnerable. Helpless. Way out of control.

Some people call it hitting bottom. I call it the crossing, where what we project on the outside meets who we are on the inside. Of course, most of us don't know who we are on the inside. We've guarded our hearts for so long that we've come to believe we are what we know—deep down—we're not.

And we don't want to go there. We don't want to be exposed. We don't want to stand at ground zero and face the stuff of life. The real stuff we've been avoiding and neglecting. Because we hate to confront. We *won't* confront.

Who wants to be like Adam and Eve and suddenly find the tree we're hiding behind is gone? And there we stand in the presence of the Lord, in the light of His glory, with fig leaves in our hands crumbling to dust.

Exposed.

It's hard to stay here.

I remember the summers during seminary when I had to do chaplaincy work. The first was at a hospital and it was hard for me. I'd go to be with a patient suffering in pain and wouldn't know what to do. So out came my rescue mode: "How can I help? What do you need? I'll get the nurse. I'll get the doctor. They'll get meds to ease your pain."

"Whose pain?" my supervisor asked. "Sounds like the one in pain was you. Sounds like you couldn't just be there with them. Pray with them. Suffer with them. Be an ambassador of Jesus Christ to them. You wanted to go for meds?"

I had to *do*. I couldn't just *be* there. It's the crossing again. Let me do, and I'm somehow still in control. Force me to just be there in their suffering, and I risk that. I risk me entering their world. To be with those in pain and do nothing? Just be there? Just feel it? Feel what it's like to cry out completely helpless, alone, afraid? And then stay there, as long as it takes?

No thanks.

Who can stand with someone at bottom and not be at bottom too? Who can weep with those suffering and still stay in control?

Don't teach me to be. Let me do. Get the meds. Numb them out. While you're at it, numb me too. Because it's true. I don't want to be here.

Of course I want to say I was there. Past tense. I've been at bottom. That's the incredible power of Christian testimony. I personally love the sheer joy of brothers and sisters in Christ getting up in the church and sharing what the Lord has done for them. They've been there. Their worlds have been torn apart. Helpless, hopeless, unable to do for themselves. Vulnerable to the forces of evil. At the very edge of despair. Suffering hardship and affliction. Feeling the hot breath of the Devil on their faces. Running deep into the valley where fear and death overpower the soul.

And then the Lord meets them, rescuing from bottom, making them safe.

And the church roars with applause. Praise to the Lord for what He has done! Yes, He allows us to be here, at the crossing, fully exposed and helpless. For it is here where we meet Jesus Christ. Where He changes lives. Where the cross is. Dug into the earth's soil. It's the only place to go to be saved, forgiven, and set free.

But we don't stay here. We never stay here.

That's the whole point, isn't it? He rescues us from places like that. He would never make us stay there. Not there. Doesn't He want us to be like we were? Shields up, defenses in place, back in control, guarding the heart? This is the Christian message I like.

The one I don't like goes like this: We never leave here. We stay here. We build our homes here. We build our churches here. Why? Because this is where Jesus Christ is. At ground zero. Where *real* is. No more Eden trees to hide behind. No more fig leaves. No more dividing walls between

what we project and who we are. No more games pretending
we are what we know we're not. No more meds or drink to
numb out. No more busy-busy doing so we don't have time
to face ourselves. No more running from the call of Jesus
Christ.

He said it plain. Clear. Unmistakable. Unavoidable.

"If anyone wishes to come after Me, he must deny himself, and take up his cross daily and follow Me. For whoever
wishes to save his life will lose it, but whoever loses his
life for My sake, he is the one who will save it" (Luke
9:23–24).

Stay here. Where we are exposed. Vulnerable. Helpless.
Way out of control. Where we have to depend upon the
Lord, trust in the Lord, every day. Where in our weakness,
His grace is sufficient. Because it is. Where we can be with
others who suddenly find themselves here. In the terrifying
sufferings of this world. Ambassadors of the Holy Spirit.

Here we are.

Where the Lord Jesus Christ presides. Where disciples
are made. Where the kingdom of God is made real.

O Lord, help me stay here.

QUESTIONS FOR REFLECTION

How good are you at staying in places where you feel
out of control?

Do you know something about meeting Jesus at ground
zero?

3

I KNOW I SAY NO

Reflections on Psalm 23

*Even though I walk through the valley of the
shadow of death, I fear no evil, for You are with me;
Your rod and Your staff, they comfort me.*

—PSALM 23:4

Testimonies are born here—where it hurts, where people suffer, where all we can do is cry out to God for help because there's nowhere else to go. Here. Stand here. Never leave here.

It's where our Lord is.

Listen to the stories. They are all the same. Every one of them gets to Easter morning the same way—through the cross. We can't avoid suffering, not in this world. Eventually, we're going to find ourselves here in need of a Savior. Because we're lost. We're scared. We need help. We need Him.

Here. He meets us here.

Even our children who grow up in Christian homes know the story. They say their prayers. They live the life. But eventually a day comes and they do what we all do. They enter the "valley of the shadow of death" (Ps. 23:4). They know about evil, but suddenly they feel it. They feel the fear of it. The power of it.

The rod, the staff, the Shepherd—no longer just a story in the Bible.

It's real. In a place called real. Where we find inside us the deepest cry the soul can ever cry: Are you real? Really real?

Testimonies are born here.

But not just testimonies. This is the exact place where discipleship happens. Where we grow up in Christ day by day, all our days. It's here where we don't play games. Where we keep our hearts open to Him. Our minds set on Him. Our wills given, in full surrender, to do what He's calling us to do.

Discipleship.

I sat across the table, sipping my coffee. The pastor and I went out for breakfast to catch up. I was visiting his church and this gave us an opportunity to enjoy each other's company and talk openly about the stuff of our lives. Inevitably, we stumbled into one of the most pressing theological issues of our day.

At some point, I shook my head and laughed a little. He asked why.

"Because it's amazing to me," I said, "what seminary did to us. We become doctors of the mind and not the soul. We forget that the truth of God's Word is intended to move from the mind so as to touch the heart. To impact us. To bring us to the place where we meet Christ and He meets us."

"It's my biggest defense!" he crowed.

"What is?"

"My mind. I thank God for seminary. It taught me how to build a fortress around my heart so I never have to deal with it. Or with anybody else's for that matter. It's how I protect myself when I'm in the middle of people's suffering. I pull out the right quote from the Bible. I tell the right story from Christian history. I give them the right answer."

"Well done us," I lamented, admiring his honest sarcasm.

"But it's all too true," he confessed. "It's how I preach. It's how I lead Bible classes. I find myself discipling Christians in just the same way. Building fortresses. Stockpiling right answers. Filling the mind with all kinds of great knowledge but never speaking to their hearts. Never entering into their pain."

And with that, somehow, we were there. At that place.

He opened up. For just a moment, the fortress walls came down. His heart was a mess. And there was good reason for it. Things of the past were crushing him, controlling him, dictating every part of his life. And he knew it. He knew it was the cause of his physical and emotional issues. He knew it was affecting his wife, his kids, and the church. But more, so much more, it distanced him from the Lord.

"It's been this way for years," he said.

"So why don't you do something about it?" I asked.

"Don't need to. I'm so good at what I do, no one really knows. Not really. Except my wife. And it's easier this way. To be honest, I'm afraid of what would happen to me if I go there. I'm afraid I'll lose my job. Afraid people will find me out. Afraid of what people will think of me."

And then he paused. Like he knew he had no choice.

"But I'll do it," he promised.

"What do you mean?"

"I mean I'll go there. I know I've been avoiding it. I know it's what the Lord wants me to do. A couple of times in my life I've sought counsel from people I thought could help but it just didn't work. So I stopped. I didn't press it. But I should have. Especially me."

"Why especially you?"

"Because I'm a pastor. My job, like you said, is to be a doctor of the soul and not just a doctor of the mind. But look at me! I pay no attention to my soul. I spend all my time avoiding the very thing I know I need to do and it's killing me inside. It's killing my relationship with the Lord. And I know it."

"Can I help?" I asked.

"Yeah. Call me in a month. Call me in two. Ask me if I've started. I know I say yes to this today, but I know myself well enough that tomorrow morning nothing will change. That's my fear. So call me."

"But why won't things change?" I asked, puzzled.

"Because I know I say yes to the Lord today. Yes to you. Yes to my wife. But when it comes time to actually do it?"

He paused. He put his head down. He said it slow. He said it real.

"I know I say no."

QUESTIONS FOR REFLECTION

Do you know what you're saying no to and when you need to say yes?

Are there Christians in your life who can help you live into that yes?

4

HE DIGS DOWN DEEP

Reflections on Hebrews 12:1–3

*And let us run with endurance the race that is
set before us, fixing our eyes on Jesus.*

—HEBREWS 12:1–2

She had gone to a place she'd never been before.
Lonely. Empty. Dark.

It's different living in a developing country, in rural Africa,
where poverty was the only life she knew. Where the basic
needs of food, clean water, security, and health care were
always in question. Add to that, she grew up under military
rule where news of killings in the villages was common.

But it wasn't different too. Her family was Christian.
They didn't turn to the occult or the worship of dead ancestors
or the easy out of alcohol. The East African Revival of the
1930s had swept into her family. Every Sunday they spent
the day in church. She grew up knowing Jesus.

At the age of twenty-three, she could honestly say she
lived a happy life. She adored her father—a common man,
a hard-working man, a devoted Christian man who always
taught her to turn to the Lord in everything. He taught her

to pray, to love the Bible, to go to God no matter what happens in life.

She loved him so much. She dreamed of marrying a man as faithful and kind as her dad, living in a modest home nearby, raising her children, tending the gardens for food, and having her kids grow up knowing their granddad. And loving him as much as she did.

Dreams that would never come true.

He left for work one morning. Kissed his wife and children, like he did every morning, got on his bicycle and took off down the road. They didn't see anything . . . or hear anything. Not until the neighbors came.

Eyewitnesses were there. They said military soldiers were driving down the road in a camouflage truck. They saw a man on a bicycle and stopped. They stopped for no reason. They stopped because it was fun.

They forced him off his bike. Taunted him. Then struck him once. Laughing like drunkards laugh. Poking him with the butts of their guns. Playing with him like a cat plays with a mouse before the kill. Then they struck him again . . . and again.

He didn't resist, they said. There was nothing he could do. They surrounded him. It happened so fast.

Again and again. Until the game was over.

And they tossed his dead body in the back of the truck and drove off. They didn't give the family the decency of seeing him. Or caring for him. Or giving him an honorable burial. Or ever knowing what happened to his body.

They never saw him again.

And her world collapsed.

Random violence. Meaningless, senseless murder. They stole her father from her. But they stole her too. Her soul went black. Like someone had the power to turn off the lights. Leaving her there. Lonely. Empty. Dark.

Moving. Functioning. Living but dead. Doing what needed to be done—for her mom, for her brothers and sisters. Because she had to. Because her dad would expect her to. Because it didn't matter. Nothing mattered. Not now, not ever.

They killed him. For no reason. Like swatting a mosquito. And they killed her too. But she still had to live every day, her heart tormented by the memory of what they did to the best man she'd ever known. And then making her live. In a world without him.

She tried to pray. She tried to go to church. Tried to do what her father had taught her to do. Tried to believe as her father had believed. But she couldn't. It's not like she was angry with God. It went deeper than that. And worse, far worse. She couldn't feel anything at all for a month. A year. Two years.

Not until an older Christian woman took her aside.

"She prayed with me," she said. "She prayed the peace of Jesus Christ would pour way down deep into my soul and fill me. Fill me so completely that the emptiness would be gone and that I'd know my Lord was there. In my hurt. My grief. My loneliness. And that I'd never be lonely again. All afternoon she prayed for me. And all these years later, I look back and remember that day as the day I knew that Jesus Christ is truly my Lord. That He met me in the deepest place of my soul and has never left. That He is everything to me and I love Him with all my heart."

It's not that she doesn't still miss her father. She does. Every day. It's not that she understands why the Lord allowed him to die such a cruel death. Or why his body was not buried with dignity. Or why some of her siblings turned away from the Lord after that—and remain turned away, at least for now. And why she didn't too.

But she always remembers what her father taught her. The world is full of trouble. Trials come, and they come hard. And no matter what happens in life, we always do what He taught us to do.

Go to Him. No matter what happens. Go to Him.

And she remembers what Jesus said. There are Christians who think they are Christians. But when trouble comes or trials or testing, they turn from Him.

"We think we know Him," she told me. "I thought I knew Him. But it was only on the surface. After my father was killed, I realized it wasn't completely true. I didn't know Him in the depths of my soul. And I didn't know His promise. He meets us there. He promises to meet us in the pain. He digs deep. He always digs down deep."

QUESTIONS FOR REFLECTION

Have you ever—in the darkest of times—turned away from the Lord rather than to Him?

What happens to you when the "why did this happen" questions aren't answered the way you need them to be answered?

5

PASSOVER EYES

Reflections on Luke 22:54–62

The Lord turned and looked at Peter.

—LUKE 22:61

I get afraid.

Sitting at the airport, waiting to fly. Too many storms in the area. Too many storms where I'm supposed to go. Already people have died. Tornadoes, high winds, flash floods—the worst storm in three years, some reports say. Three days marching across the south.

My 3:25 flight delayed till 4:00.

I stare out the terminal windows. At 3:45, the already dark skies turn black . . . angry. Lightning, thunder, visibility gone. Water streaming down the floor-to-ceiling windows. The lights flickering on and off. A few miles away a twister hits ground. A hundred people at a Lowes hardware store huddle in a safe place as the building around them collapses.

Flight delayed till 5:30.

I sit in the Raleigh airport not knowing that sixty-two tornadoes are touching down in North Carolina this afternoon.

Twenty-three people are dying. One tornado, in Bertie County just east of Raleigh, tore a path of six miles. Sixty-five homes destroyed, six hundred damaged. In a matter of minutes, eleven die, fifty plus injured.

Delayed till 7:15.

I'm trying to get to New York. I get a text from my family back home. High winds already started, rains coming. Warnings of flash floods show on the TV. The news reports that forty-five people have died from the storm over three days in six states, 230 recorded twisters.

I wonder what I should do. I don't like the way it feels.

I watch the people around me. Some are deciding to leave, book a hotel, rebook their flights for the morning. Stay safe.

Delayed again till 9:45.

I had just spent three days teaching at a church nearby. It began Thursday night when fourteen people stood to renew their commitment to Jesus Christ. Yesterday and today, I was able to meet with staff, clergy, and church elders. I heard testimony after testimony of the Lord's saving power in people's lives. Rescue in the midst of despair. Hope even when the world turns upside down.

I think about the stories now. I think about the words I said as I taught from the Bible. And then I think about the fear inside me and wonder if I'm not so unlike the apostle Peter. He was so confident, so strong, when he said, "Lord, with You I am ready to go both to prison and to death!" (Luke 22:33).

But the testing came in full force. And his confidence turned to ashes. Fear took over and Peter fell to it, denying the Lord three times. Is that me? And what was it like for Peter to hear the rooster crow? But worse, a thousand times worse, the Lord heard the rooster too and He looked for Peter (see Luke 23:34). Until He found him. "The Lord turned and looked at Peter" (Luke 22:61).

Those eyes, looking straight at Peter, knowing what he'd done.

I feel those same eyes looking at me. Here, now, as I stand in the airport, as lightning dances around me. I was so confident as I taught the Bible these past three days. Now look at me! Once so confident, so strong, now so full of fear.

Delayed again. No news till after 10:30.

The pilot stands alone. I go over to talk to him. He shows me the radar over New York. The big green blob of rain everywhere. The yellow masses inside of thunder cells. The red inside them warning of severe winds, possible tornadoes.

He asks me what I do. I tell him I am a clergyman. That I was hoping to get back tonight for the Palm Sunday service in the morning at my home church. He tells me about his son, Bryan, twenty-one years old, at full stride in life, in college, with all kinds of possibilities in front of him. Until one night last August. He was at a party, sitting on a wall, and accidently fell backwards some ten to twelve feet, severing his spinal cord. A paraplegic for life.

"Eight months later," he says, his eyes sad, "and he's scared. He's depressed. He's lost hope. It breaks my heart. I don't know what to do for him."

The more we talk, the more I hear his heart for his son.

I immediately want to do something for him. I know I'll never see him again. I remember a website, a place to go where the Christian witness is strong for those suffering paralysis. I tell him about it. I tell him I'll pray for his son, Bryan. And for him.

Nothing, I say, has helped me more than being with Christians who breathe hope and meaning into my life. I tell him I want that for Bryan. He nods and shakes my hand.

We take off at 11:20 at night.

At midnight, we began the descent into New York and into the storm. The jet tossed and jerked up and around by the force of the winds. The babies and little children were crying. Lightning flashed on the right side. Close enough to touch.

Thirty minutes left till we land.

I think about the forty-five already killed by this storm—those who heard the tornado coming, who did what they could to find shelter. I think about the mother who lost her baby in a flash flood. I think about Bryan. And those who know this fear like I know it now.

I think about Peter again—my mind frantic—and wonder what was it like that night when the cock crowed and Peter saw the Lord seeing him? All he could do was run, weeping bitterly. I can't imagine it. And more, what was it like to see Him that Passover night, to look into His eyes. He was already there. Already bound. Already descending into the storm of all storms. What was it like for Him? Had the sin of the world already come upon Him? Did He know something about this fear as the thunders of death encircled him? Was it in His eyes?

The jet keeps jerking. My heart keeps racing. And all I can think about are those eyes of His. Him looking at me and seeing my fear. Me looking at Him and seeing His.

Those eyes of His. Those Passover eyes.

QUESTIONS FOR REFLECTION

Have you ever felt fear so great that you said and did what you knew you shouldn't?

Do you know what it's like to be sure of what you believe and suddenly so unsure when testing comes?

6
CRUSTED HARD

Reflections on Matthew 21:28–32

*For John came to you in the way of righteousness
and you did not believe him; but the tax collectors and
prostitutes did believe him; and you, seeing this, did not
even feel remorse afterward so as to believe him.*

—MATTHEW 21:32

On Good Friday, when He died, the veil was torn, the earth shook, the rocks split. Tombs were opened and a centurion said, "This man was the Son of God" (Mark 15:39; see also Matt. 27:51–54).

Why the centurion? Of all people. Why not the religious leaders of the day? Why does Jesus say to the chief priests and elders that "tax collectors and prostitutes will get into the kingdom of God" before them (Matt. 21:31)?

These people? Of all people.

I remember meeting a man once. Big, hard worker. Gruff. What he did, he did well. He cared about his work. Didn't really care about people though. What they thought of him. What they said about him.

I got to spend some time with him. I found out that he was bumped from foster home to foster home growing up. He never knew his real dad. He found his real mom and still talks to her a couple times a year, just so she knows he's alive. But that's about it. He's never really had anyone care about him. No sense of ever being loved, protected, valued. He has no real friendships to speak of. Not in his past, not now. He treats people the way he's been treated. And that's the problem. He hurts people by his words and actions. What for most people is morally wrong isn't for him. He runs over people and doesn't look back. Like it never happened.

"Ever gone to church?" I asked him one day.

"You kiddin' me?" he laughed. "Never been. Never want to."

"Because you don't believe in God?"

He shrugged his shoulders and changed the subject.

I didn't push. Nor did I pretend to understand his world. I didn't. But I sort of got his story. His drinking. His drug use. His first marriage. His second marriage. Girlfriend here, girlfriend there. But no relationships over two or three years.

He curses life, especially his life.

He knows he's bitter. His heart cold as ice and crusted hard.

I'm not sure why I was allowed to be there when it happened. But I'll never forget it. It was a beautiful summer, Saturday afternoon. A picnic in the park. Food, a band, tons of people, children playing, young people tossing Frisbees.

One of the guys in the band introduced a speaker, a man in his thirties, who came up and grabbed the microphone. He began to talk and most people stopped to listen to him.

He told story after story about his life. He'd been hit hard by circumstances that plunged him into the gutter of despair and to the edge of suicide. And it almost worked. If it hadn't been for a friend. Someone who told him about Jesus Christ.

And something caught my eye as he talked. In the crowd of people, I saw him. My friend. He was there. Why was he there? And he was listening. Why was he listening?

I decided, after the speaker finished, to go and talk to my friend. I expected him to laugh it off and mock the man's story of what Jesus Christ had done in his life. Instead, I found tears in his eyes. Real tears. Crazy, out-of-control tears. He said he was sorry. He tried to stop and push it away but it didn't work. The more he tried, the more he cried.

"It's like I can feel God is right here with me," he said.

"Yeah," I replied. I did my best to explain what was happening to him. I told him about the Holy Spirit. I told him the first thing He does when He comes is to reveal God to us. And then He shows us our sin. Our pride. Our rebellion.

"It's called His convicting power. It's what He does," I told him. (See John 16:7–15.)

He nodded his head. Somehow that made sense to him. And then he said he wanted more because it felt so right, so clean. Like all the junk of his life was being washed away. He said he felt sorry for what he had done. Sorry for all the people he hurt and pain he caused. Sorry until his words turned to prayer.

"Jesus, Lord, have mercy on me. Please have mercy on me."

I sat with him like a spectator on the sidelines. Like it was Good Friday here and now. The earth shaking. The rocks splitting. This man's tomb opened wide. He was alive in Jesus. And his heart was crusted hard no more. Made new by the grace, kindness, and power of the Holy Spirit.

This man, my friend. Of all people.

I've never understood it. Why tax collectors and prostitutes, addicts and criminals, those beaten down and trashed by life, suddenly come alive and leap into the kingdom of God.

Or why when this happened to me, when Jesus Christ changed my life, I ran to the people in my church, and to my pastor. I told them what had happened to me. And I thought they'd say, "Finally! Now he gets it!"

But no, it wasn't like that. They thought something was wrong with me. And it confused me. It still confuses me. Why people so close to God can be so far from Him. And why those so far from Him end up being so close.

Of all people.

Who really are the crusted hard?

QUESTIONS FOR REFLECTION

Are you—of all people—one of the crusted hard?

Why do people tend to run away from the kind of people Jesus runs to? Do you?

7

WHOLE

Reflections on John 4:7–30

Jesus said to her, "I who speak to you am He."
—JOHN 4:26

There's somewhere to go. Something to do.

It was after service. I was preaching on a Sunday morning at a church in New England, still in my late twenties. Standing in the back of the church, a young woman gave me the tiniest glimpse into her life. She wanted me to know, more than anything, that she had met Jesus. That He was everything to her. That her life was different today because of Him.

I asked how it happened.

At first, she made general comments. Her life had been hard. She had lost her way. She got in with the wrong crowd. She did things she shouldn't have. But as she talked, she went deeper. She'd fallen prey to a man who dominated her—abused her, hooked her on drugs, and then threw her into the world of prostitution where night after night she felt raped and tortured. She said she tried to run twice. Both times he found her and told her he'd kill her.

"I didn't know," she said, "if I was dying or if I was already dead."

Her eyes filled with tears as she talked. She couldn't have been more than twenty-five. Still, there was a gentleness about her.

"The police busted the guy," she went on. "I was in prison for a few months. More like detox. When my head cleared, I just wanted to die. I felt like a piece of trash. So dirty and ugly inside. So embarrassed and filled with shame. What was I supposed to do when I got out of prison? Where would I go?"

And then she said something I'll never forget. It changed something inside of me. It was more than just a word, more than a feeling, need, or craving of the heart. There was something deeper here.

"I wanted one thing. Just one thing," she said. "I wanted to be whole."

That's not what I was expecting her to say. I thought she was going to say, "I wanted to be clean."

Clean. That's the word. That's the picture of baptism. That's what John the Baptist was doing in the Jordan. He was inviting people to come down. Down into the waters of repentance. Down and under—to receive forgiveness of sin.

To wash. Real washing. Washing on the inside.

Like the woman at the well in John 4. She met Jesus. And Jesus met her. She didn't have to tell Him her story. She didn't need to reveal the pain in her life. The men. The abuse. The deepest harshest feelings of being ravaged and filthy in soul. Somehow He already knew. He knew it all.

And He talked of living water. This confused her.

It can confuse the reader too. We don't see it. We only hear about it. If we take it, hold it, and drink it, it becomes in us "a well of water springing up to eternal life" (John 4:14). Great news, but where is it? Why doesn't He give it to her?

But He does. We have to have eyes to see it. It's there. As they're talking, this moment happens when she asks about the coming of the Messiah and that He, when He comes, will "declare all things to us" (John 4:25).

And that's it. He hands her the living water. Not with a wooden spoon dipped into the well, but with words. Words bigger than words. Words that speak power to the soul. Power to wash. Power to clean the dirt. The filth. The stains that are so deep inside we think nothing in the world has the power to make it go away.

"I who speak to you am He" (John 4:26).

And the woman drinks.

Then she runs to the city. She tells them all. She's different inside. She knows it. They know it. They know it enough to believe her. Enough to follow her. And to let her lead them to Jesus.

I've always seen this moment as a kind of baptism. Her washing inside. Like the apostle Paul said to the Corinthians, "But you were washed . . . in the name of the Lord Jesus Christ and in the Spirit of our God" (1 Cor. 6:11).

Washed clean on the inside. All that dirt of our sin gone. All the filth of what people have done to hurt us, abuse us, shame us—gone.

But it's more.

The woman I met that day at the back of the church taught me that. She told me she met Jesus. And Jesus met her. She told me how it happened and all the details that surrounded that day. But as she spoke, it was like she was taking me to the well.

Like there was somewhere to go. Something to do.

To take the water. Hold it. Drink it. Go down into it. That there's power here.

The power of what Jesus Christ did for us on the cross. Power to forgive our sins. Power to wash the un-washable stains forever from the heart and soul.

"He did all that for me," she said. "And so much more."

And then she told me the burden of her heart. So many women just like her. Battered and beaten, day after day, with nowhere to go, nothing they could do. Feeling vulnerable, helpless and trapped.

"I want to find them," she told me. "I want them to know Jesus. I want them to know that what He did for me He will do for them."

And then she said it simply: "He will make them safe. And then, after that, He will make them whole."

QUESTIONS FOR REFLECTION

Are there places in you that need to be clean?
Are there places in you that need to be whole?

8

AND THE JOURNEY BEGINS

Reflections on Mark 1:1–8

*And he was preaching, and saying, "After me One is
coming who is mightier than I, and I am not fit to
stoop down and untie the thong of His sandals."*

—MARK 1:7

Sometimes I want to break into a passage in the Bible
and be there, like a reporter covering the scene. Cameras,
microphones, the works. I'd start at the Jordan. With the
Baptist. I'd ask the obvious questions. His clothing. His
food. His hair. Where he sleeps. What he owns. Why he's
chosen a life of poverty. Then I'd get down to business. I'd
ask why he hangs out with the poor. Why the people all
around him are outcasts, sinners, prostitutes, tax collectors.

Those kinds of people.

I think it was 1964. We were northerners living in the
South. Dad had been transferred by his company. We only
stayed there three years.

Mom hired Florence to come and help her around the
house. An incredibly kind African-American woman, who
fit perfectly into our family. To this day, I can remember
the sound of her voice and her little, unforgettable sayings.

It felt good, comfortable, to have her in our world.

But one night we got in the car, drove across town, and entered hers.

We went to her church. Something festive was happening that night. A special service of some kind. Maybe it was for one of Florence's children? Were they raising money for something? I can't remember. All I know is that we stuck out huge. Very, very white faces in a sea of dark faces.

I didn't feel scared. I felt different. Everything was different. Our church wasn't like this. We didn't sing like that. We didn't talk like that. We didn't dress like that. We were formal, white, upper middle class, barely knowing anybody's name. These people were poor. Everybody knowing everybody.

We found our way to a row of chairs near the front before the service began. And then Florence appeared. Her smile welcoming us. A beautiful joy on her face.

I was seven. I didn't understand the tension between North and South. White and black. Rich and poor. Favored and less-than-favored. Us kinds of people and those kinds of people.

But I felt it. I felt the divide. I knew we were visiting, for one night. And that we wouldn't come back. We weren't church shopping. We were there because we loved Florence and we wanted to bless her like she was blessing us.

Then rush home. Back to our world. And we never went back.

But there was something about that night I'll never forget. An image, if I close my eyes, I can still see. Up front, an altar rail packed with people kneeling. And Florence was there. Kneeling before the Lord. Her elbows resting on the rail, her hands clasped in front of her. Her head bowed. Praying.

In a world of differences, this was the same.

We did that too at church. The altar rail. Kneeling before the Lord. Our heads bowed. Praying to the same Lord she was praying to. Same One.

So it's simple, I thought. When we kneel, we're the same. When we stand up and face each other, our worlds split and divide.

Us kinds of people. Those kinds of people.

Don't fool yourself. The Baptist came from family. High society. His dad was a priest of the Most High God, with status, and position, blameless before God (Luke 1:5–7).

So ask the questions: Why is this up-scale guy hanging out with the poor, outcast, marginalized, and even worse than that—the wicked and immoral? Why break into their world and stay?

At first, I expect the normal answer: Because that's what we're supposed to do. We're supposed to go to those in need and be there for them. Be one of them, but don't be. There, but separate. The split and divide always present.

But that's not John.

He's the one who said, "I am not fit to stoop down and untie the thong of His sandals" (Mark 1:7). Why did he say that? I believe it's because his eyes were fixed on the glory and majesty of his coming Lord. For this reason, John bent low.

Everyone in that day knew the only person to stoop down and untie the thong of a sandal was a slave. The lowest of the low. The marginalized and outcast. And here John said he wasn't fit—he didn't even qualify—to be the lowest of the low.

Not in the presence of the Lord of glory.

John was lower still.

Like Florence kneeling before her Lord.

Where all our differences turn to powdered dust. No more us kinds of people and those kinds of people. No more seeing each other as rich or poor, white or black, educated or not, beautiful or not, in the center of society or marginalized to the outskirts, moral or immoral.

Here on our knees, we are the same.

That's what happens to us in Jesus. Us kinds and those kinds become one kind. All following Jesus Christ. All learning to become His disciples in the midst of a broken, fallen world of splits and divides. All of us. On our knees. One family bent low before the Lord of glory.

And the journey begins.

QUESTIONS FOR REFLECTION

Is it possible to identify the splits and divides in your life?

What would happen to us if we bent low to everyone we knew and everyone we met?

PART 2

IDENTITY
IN JESUS

9

TAKING FIRST STEPS

Reflections on Matthew 28:16–20

Go therefore and make disciples of all the nations.
—MATTHEW 28:19

I sat at lunch with a good friend a few months ago. I had just finished some writing on what it means to be a disciple of Jesus Christ, and I wanted to talk to him about it. The more we talked, the more he dug.

"Sounds like you're trying to stir passion in people's hearts to be intentional disciples of our Lord," he remarked.

I'd brought with me a couple of newly published books. One was Eugene Peterson's *Practice Resurrection*.

"Look at this," I said. "Peterson's calling us to 'the work of the Holy Spirit forming our born-again spirits into the likeness of Christ.'[1] His challenge, as he takes us through Ephesians, is to call us to live godly lives in Christ and to 'walk in a manner worthy of the Lord' (Col. 1:10; see also Eph. 4:1).

"It's a lot more than just believe right, to think right," I added. "The Lord wants us to be right so we can walk right."

My friend sat back.

He hadn't read Peterson's book yet, but he had read Dallas Willard's *The Great Omission*, as well as John Stott's last work, *The Radical Disciple*. These great Christian leaders from varied traditions all echoed the same concern: The church worldwide may be growing in numbers but, sadly, it's "growth without depth." We're suffering in character from a "lack of godliness and integrity."[2]

"I agree," he said strongly. "If the Lord doesn't do this work in us, in our hearts and minds, we have no hope of impacting our world for Christ. But . . ."

"But what?"

"But something's missing," he challenged.

"What do you mean?"

"You can't stir passion for something and then not show us how it's done. You've got to give us more. We need first steps. We need to know what it looks like. Map it out for us. Show us where to start."

I looked at him confused. I just didn't understand.

"If I want to be a disciple of Jesus Christ," he said emphatically, "if I want to be conformed to His image, if I want to see the Holy Spirit do His work in me so everyday I'm walking worthy of Him, I need to know how to do that."

Caught.

I hate this about me. I hate that I focus on the upfront sell. Motivate, inspire, excite people in seeing what's possible in Jesus Christ. Get them to make the commitment to follow Him with all their heart, mind, and soul. And that's that. Off they go. Off I go. I don't stick around. I don't do the hard work with them. I stay too safe.

It reminded me of a flight I took to Washington, D.C., a few years ago. I was sitting next to a businessman, a Roman Catholic, who told me the joy he and his wife felt as they watched their daughter learn the Lord's Prayer.

"She's got her first Communion coming up and we're thrilled," he told me.

I asked him what he did. He told me he worked with companies to implement high-end software.

"Companies always want to be on the leading edge with technology," he said. "It makes them more efficient and, therefore, more competitive. So they bid out for the best product at the best price. Salespeople do their little dance until one of them wins the contract. And that's where I come in."

"To do what?" I asked.

"You see, too many companies buy the product because it's the right thing to do. But then nothing happens. It just sits on the shelf gathering dust because no one takes the time to learn the software and integrate it into their systems. That's where we come in. We help make it happen. We work with their people until they're fluent in the new software."

Caught.

I told him we were in the same business. But I was honest with him. I told him I was a clergyman and that I tend to be the dancing salesman more than the guy who helps people walk into the "new software" step by step.

"Tell me what you mean," he inquired.

"Well, it's like your daughter," I said. "You're teaching her the Lord's Prayer so she knows it word for word. But what about the application? Now there's the challenge! We say, 'Thy will be done.' But how do we do that? How do we live our lives so that we're living in His will, His plan for us day by day, and not our own?"

"Ouch!" he said. "That's not something my wife and I have ever talked about."

"Well, let me say 'Ouch!' back. Because you've help me see what's really important here. I've got to do more of what you do in my church. Less selling. More applying." I felt, at that moment, quite convicted of my sin and selfishness. Caught in always playing it too safe.

My friend at lunch smiled at this story.

I grabbed my iced tea and stated the obvious. "I guess it's time to stop talking about it—and just do it! What do you think?"

"You got it! Help us take first steps," he encouraged. "Give us more."

QUESTIONS FOR REFLECTION

Why is it is easier to talk about what we believe than to live what we believe?

What do you think would change if you started to pray daily, "Lord, teach me to apply Your Word to my life"?

NOTES

1. Eugene H. Peterson, *Practice Resurrection: A Conversation on Growing Up in Christ* (Grand Rapids, Mich.: Eerdmans, 2010), 2.

2. John Stott, *The Radical Disciple: Some Neglected Aspects of Our Calling* (Downers Grove, Ill.: InterVarsity Press, 2010), 39.

10

WHERE TO START

Reflections on Psalm 139:1–14

*For You formed my inward parts; You wove me
in my mother's womb. I will give thanks to You,
for I am fearfully and wonderfully made; wonderful
are Your works, and my soul knows it very well.*

—PSALM 139:13–14

We pulled into their driveway about 6:30 p.m. We were
so excited to see them and their new home. They did their
best to welcome us, but from the moment we saw them, we
knew something was wrong. Really wrong.

"You OK?" I asked my friend. He'd been in ministry for
years and had just accepted a call to pastor a church nearby.

"Not really," he admitted. "We've got something to show
you." And with that, he, his wife, and both their children
marched us down to their basement which had a finished
room on one side and a garage on the other.

"What do you think?" he asked, as we walked into the
garage.

"It looks great," I said, especially as I noticed a large,
banner-wide painting stretching across the entire back wall.

"It's crazy," his wife said, "we did all the inspections
before buying the house. Everything checked out. The

house isn't even twenty years old. The people who sold it to us couldn't have been nicer."

My friend waved me over to help him take the painting off the wall. "Look at that!" he exclaimed.

Behind the painting was a large crack, shaped like a lightning bolt, dug deep into the foundation. It was long, a few inches wide, and devastating to see.

"Oh, I'm so sorry," my wife said softly.

"Somebody knew about this," my friend determined, "and covered it up with the painting. The house is now legally ours which means so is the problem."

"So, what are you going to do?" I asked.

"We've had a few people come out and look at it, and they all say the same thing. They're going to have to lift the house off its foundation, tear out the old one and lay a new foundation like they're starting from scratch."

"They can do that?"

"They say they can. But it takes time and money—a lot of money."

We all stood there, staring at the crack, wondering how it happened and how anyone could go to such lengths to cover it up. Such dishonesty and greed.

After dinner, our friends reflected on the story.

"At first, I was angry," the pastor started. "I still am. But I can't help thinking the Lord will use this in a profound way at our church."

"What do you mean?" I asked.

"We came here knowing the church was in trouble. For years, it was doing great. It was healthy, robust, and deeply impacting the local community for Christ. The pastor died eight years ago and since then, nothing has worked."

"They've had two pastors since," his wife picked up. "There've been disputes among the elders over little things that drove people away and the ones who stayed just want their church back to the way things were."

"We're about half the size as eight years ago," her husband stated. "There's no question, we need the Lord to visit this church again."

"And you knew all this before you came?" I asked.

"We sure did. But we didn't know the severity of the problem," he responded. "And I think that's where the story of our house connects."

"How?" my wife asked.

"We think it's possible that what the Lord is doing with our house may be exactly what He wants to do at the church. He wants to get at the foundation. Tear out the old and lay down the new just like the apostle Paul said to the Corinthians, 'According to the grace of God which was given to me, like a wise master builder I laid a foundation . . . which is Jesus Christ'" (1 Cor. 3:10–11).

"So I guess that means you lift up the house," I said, bewildered at the thought of it, "and start building as if you're building for the first time."

"Exactly," he nodded.

"Well, I can tell you what I do when I start meeting with new Christians," my wife added and then smiled. "I always go to Psalm 139."

"Why there?" the pastor asked.

"Because it's where it all starts. It's the beginning. It helps us ask the two most important questions anyone can ask: Who is God, and who am I? And I love the way the psalm speaks to it: 'For You formed my inward parts; You wove me in my mother's womb. I will give thanks to You, for I am fearfully and wonderfully made; wonderful are Your works, and my soul knows it very well' (Ps. 139:13–14). Now that, to me, is the beginning!" she exclaimed. "To know I'm not an accident. That I was planned by God. Created and loved by God. Fearfully and wonderfully made by Him who is my heavenly Father. And that who I am, my real and true identity, doesn't start with me, or my broken world, or people who've hurt me. It all starts with God first. He's the focal point. This is always step one! It's where the work on the foundation begins."

"As long as I've known you," the pastor's wife said with delight, "you've always gone back to the beginning. Back to Genesis 1. Back to being made in God's image."

"Well," my wife said teasingly, "if you're going to go to all the trouble of lifting up the house to get at the foundation, you might as well do what God did and start at the beginning!"

We all laughed, but we knew the seriousness of it. Before the night was over, we spent time in prayer for the work on the house, the work at the church, and asked the Lord to work on us first—whatever needs to be done—that He begin with us.

QUESTIONS FOR REFLECTION

Are there cracks in the foundation of your life, covered so no one can see?

Do you know you are not an accident, but planned and wanted by God?

11

WHO ARE YOU, LORD? WHO AM I?

Reflections on Psalm 139:15–24

*My frame was not hidden from You, when I was made in secret,
and skillfully wrought in the depths of the earth; Your eyes have seen
my unformed substance; and in Your book were all written the days
that were ordained for me, when as yet there was not one of them.*

—PSALM 139:15–16

Dame Cicely Saunders died on July 14, 2005, at the age of eighty-seven. A remarkable woman who will long be remembered. What she did has hugely impacted our world for the better.

What she did wasn't who she was. That didn't come first.

She first belonged to Jesus Christ. In 1945 after the divorce of her parents, Cicely Saunders converted from agnosticism to Christianity. It was based on this faith in the Lord that she prayed to know how best to serve God. She believed He had a plan for her life, that He was in control of her days, and that He knew her intimately, as Psalm 139:15–16 says.

Too often in life, we think the exact opposite. We are what we do. Our identity is wrapped up in our achievements: what schools we've attended, degrees we've earned, jobs we've held, places we've traveled, people we've known, power we've wielded, or possessions we've accrued.

But we are not what we do. That's a lie from the Devil.

We are first people created by God for God. Our identity is first found in Him. Our value. Our worth. Our meaning. Our purpose in life comes second, always second. Because we can't know what He's called us to do until we first know He created us and called us to Himself, for Himself.

We belong to Him.

That's where we find our worth. Not in what we do but in Who we belong to.

This was true for Cicely Saunders. What she did in life, writes David Clark, her biographer, was "underpinned by a powerful religious commitment."[1] She wanted to serve the Lord. That was her prayer. And He answered, giving her a heart and passion for the dying. She trained as a nurse and social worker. Then, at the age of thirty-three, in a day when few women were doctors, she studied to be a doctor. So she could devote herself to the dying.

That peculiar time in life when we can't do for ourselves. When all we have is stripped away. And if our identity is wrapped up in what we do, we're in big trouble because we can't do. Not then. Not when we're dying.

But if our identity is wrapped up in Who we belong to, if our worth is found in the One who created us and called us to Himself, then everything changes. Everything! Because we matter to Him. And in Him we have worth.

Dr. Cicely Saunders dreamed the impossible dream. She wanted the dying to know the kindness and mercy of God. So she became the founder of a "worldwide movement to provide compassionate care for the dying." A movement called hospice. She said, "I didn't set out to change the world; I set out to do something about pain." Physical pain.

And heart pain. She'd tell her patients, "You matter because you are you, and you matter to the last moment of your life."[2]

You matter before God. Not just what you do. You matter because you are you.

The world around us teaches us that purpose comes first. Find purpose, find identity. Just take the simple test. Ask somebody, "Who are you?" and more times than not, they'll answer you with what they do. "I'm a school teacher . . . a lawyer . . . a salesman . . . a hockey-dad." "I'm a mom . . . a wife . . . an accountant . . . a businesswoman." I am what I do. In order to be somebody, I have to produce. And if I produce, I get to tell people that I'm somebody.

It's how the world spins. Find purpose, find identity.

As I was growing up, I remember being told that men often die after they retire. They don't know what to do with themselves. They get lost in life because all they know is what they do. And what they do is who they are. So the moment they stop doing what they do, they lose themselves.

Big, big trouble. Being a Christian changes all that.

When somebody asks, "Who are you?" we know what to say: "I'm a Christian." Or, to say it another way, "I belong to Christ." Because who we are is wrapped up completely in who He is.

We belong to Him. He made us. By God's own hand, we were "skillfully wrought in the depths of the earth." He saw our "unformed substance." In His book "were all written the days that were ordained" for us. We are "fearfully and wonderfully made" (Ps. 139:14–16).

Our identity begins and ends with God. Whether we can or can't do. Our value, our worth, our meaning, is found in our relationship with Him. Just as the good doctor, Cicely Saunders said.

You matter before God. Not just what you do. You matter because you are you.

That's how the Christian walk starts. Identity comes first. The first questions are never, "What's my purpose, Lord? What have You called me to do?" The first two questions are, "Who are You, Lord, and who am I?"

QUESTIONS FOR REFLECTION

When somebody asks you, "Who are you?" what do you say?

Is it possible that your identity is wrapped up deeply in what you do and what you've accomplished?

NOTES

1. Barbara Field, "Science Hero: Dame Cicely Saunders," The My Hero Project, last modified September 29, 2012, http://www.myhero.com/go/hero.asp?hero=Cicely_Saunders_06.

2. Ibid.

12
FINDING IDENTITY

Reflections on Genesis 1

In the beginning God created the heavens and the earth.
—GENESIS 1:1

He held his head in his hands and sobbed. He was done. So tired. So lost.

We were in the middle of a church service, and I was the visiting preacher. Sitting next to me was the associate pastor. A young man, gifted, with an extraordinary story of growing up in a secular home with no talk of God. Or church. Or prayer. Or the Bible. Or even the mention of Jesus.

College changed all that.

Without knowing it, he was surrounded by Christians everywhere: in class, at the dorm. He suddenly had new friends to hang out with and one thing led to another.

His conversion was dramatic. So dramatic that he received invitation after invitation to give his testimony in different venues. A pastor saw him, took him under his wing and put him to work in ministry as a youth pastor, then as an associate.

For ten years, he's been serving. Serving in ministry even while training for ministry. Both at the same time. Serving, constantly serving.

And then he got married. One child, then two. Then came more responsibility as the church grew, which required more of him.

Always more.

Until he broke that Sunday. He did his best to explain his broken heart. "I don't know who I am," he said. "No one has ever mentored me, discipled me, cared for me. It's always give and give. I never receive. No one has ever done that for me."

No one started him at the beginning.

So, for example, when his sister died three years ago in a car crash, no one pastored the young pastor. He didn't know what to do with his grief. At the funeral service, he was told that his sister was with Jesus and that's all he needed to know. He needed to be happy for her. So he pushed his grief down. He smiled through his tears. He buried his anger, his outrage that his sister was taken from him—so violently. So needlessly. He missed her. He longed for her.

He wanted to say to someone, "Why did this happen? Did God do this? If He didn't do it, did He allow it? Why didn't He stop it? Why didn't He protect her?" But there was no one to talk to. He didn't want to blame God but he did, secretly. Without even knowing it, he began seeing Him through the lens of his sister's death.

God. The monster who killed his sister.

Or did He?

If only someone had started him at the beginning, in the beginning. When God created the heavens and the earth. And even before that, before He ever created.

"Blessed be the God and Father of our Lord Jesus Christ, who has blessed us with every spiritual blessing in the heavenly places in Christ, just as He chose us in Him before the foundation of the world" (Eph. 1:3–4).

God. Before creation, "before the foundation of the world."

He chose us. He chose us to be in Him. Bound in relationship to Him. Not just the day we were conceived. Or the day we were born. But before time began. We were in the mind and heart of God before the beginning. This means we were not some accident of nature. Not a surprise to our parents. We were not unplanned, but planned. Not unwanted, but wanted. Not unloved, but loved. Not abandoned or rejected or tossed aside. But His. Completely His. Chosen by God, even before we read Genesis 1:1. Before He created heaven and earth, He had a plan. And His plan saw us, knew us, loved us, and chose us before time began.

God. He's not the monster we see through the lens of our suffering. He's our God and Father who "chose us in Him before the foundation of the world, that we would be holy and blameless before Him" (Eph. 1:4).

And the only way we could ever be "holy and blameless" is because He is holy and blameless. Just as all of heaven declares, "Holy, Holy, Holy, is the LORD of hosts, the whole earth is full of His glory" (Isa. 6:3).

For this reason, the Bible says, "God is Light, and in Him there is no darkness at all" (1 John 1:5). And again, "For I, the LORD, do not change" (Mal. 3:6; see also Heb. 13:8).

God. Unchanging God. God who is holy, full of glory, without darkness or imperfection.

God who is not the monster. Never the monster. Never the One to blame for the broken, fallen, terrifying world we live in. Never the creator and author of evil. Never the One we should run away from when we hurt and grieve.

But the One we run *to*. The One who created all things "very good" because God Himself is good (Gen. 1:31; see also Ps. 34:8; 86:5). Always good. Even when everything around us turns bad. This is the One who created us in His image and promised, when all things come to their perfect fulfillment, to restore us back into that image. The image of His Son (Rom. 8:29; 2 Cor. 3:18).

God.

We start here. At the beginning. We don't have all the answers. We don't know why this young pastor's sister died so tragically. But we do know where to go and Who to turn to. And rather than seeing Him through the lens of our deepest suffering, we do the exact opposite.

We see our deepest suffering through the lens of Him who is God. God the unchanging God. God the holy God. God who chose us to be with Him.

Now. Always. Forever.

QUESTIONS FOR REFLECTION

Has anyone taken time to mentor you and disciple you in the faith, or have you had to go it alone?

Are you able to believe in a God who is good, even in the midst of your losses, pain, and suffering?

13

CRAZY-CRAZY WORLD

Reflections on Genesis 3:1–7

The serpent said to the woman, "You surely will not die!"

—Genesis 3:4

The serpent appeared.

We are told he is "called the devil and Satan, who deceives the whole world" (Rev. 12:9). We are told he was once an anointed cherub, a glorious angel, who was "full of wisdom and perfect in beauty" (Ezek. 28:12–19; see also Isa. 14:12–17). We don't know how it happened, but he became filled with pride, corruption, and self-ambition and sinned in his heart against God. And because of that sin, he was "thrust down to Sheol" or hell (Isa. 14:15).

This is the one who appeared in the garden of Eden, dressed as a serpent. Who was allowed in the garden.

But be certain about this: His evil was not created by God. The Bible makes this quite clear. God did not create evil. God is, by nature, "the Father of lights" (James 1:17) in whom "there is no darkness" (1 John 1:5). He is eternally opposed to evil, sin, and corruption, and He must, without partiality by sovereign edict, bring it under His perfect judgment.

The Devil. Loose in the garden. Dressed in the disguise of an Eden serpent.

We are told he deceived Eve. We are told the man was tempted. Tempted to break God's command which said he was not to eat from one of the trees (Gen. 2:16–17; 3:17). But he did. And when he did, a dark, evil power burst in full force into the world. Just as the Bible says, "Through one man sin entered into the world, and death through sin" (Rom. 5:12). Sin that wages war in the mortal body. Death that reigns over the fallen soul. Evil that forces itself upon the whole of creation making it reel from "its slavery to corruption" (Rom. 8:21–22; see also 6:12; 7:23; Heb. 2:14–15; 1 Cor. 15:55).

And the God-made, God-perfect, God-holy world turned crazy-crazy.

A knock came on our cabin door. It was an early Tuesday morning in September 2008. So odd for us to be on vacation. We normally go in July or August. But this year, for whatever reason, was different.

"You need to call your sister," the person at the door told me. We were renting the cabin and apparently the phone lines weren't working.

I grabbed my cell phone and went out to the main street hoping to find a signal. As soon as I got it I called my sister.

Within minutes after the call, my wife and I jumped into the car and drove to a hospital in Biddeford, Maine, where my niece and her husband lived. It took one long hour to get there, park, and find our way to their hospital room.

The two of them huddled together in the bed. Holding each other. With faces swollen red from crying.

Their beautiful baby boy. Healthy and alive a few hours ago, after a perfect pregnancy.

The contractions came. Just as they do. At the right time, my niece and her husband went to the hospital. Everything as planned. Everyone so nice. Each step with a healthy dose of nervous anticipation as labor continued and the excitement mounted of seeing their first-born son.

There was no heartbeat.

From the moment they arrived at the hospital. No sound.

Later, the doctor said the child's head crushed the umbilical cord in the birth canal, cutting off the oxygen, stealing the child's life.

And the baby was born in silence.

Still.

They let me hold him. Perfect little Noah. Every feature formed. The pug little nose. The color of the hair. Tiny little finger nails. Bundled in blankets to keep him snug and safe and warm, protected from this dark, terrifying world.

A world where twenty-four thousand children died that same day of preventable causes like measles, malaria, dirty water, hunger, HIV, and natural disasters.[1]

His body was cold to my touch. His face ashen.

His parents want a do-over. They want to replay the story, leap back in time, back twenty-four hours and demand an immediate C-section. Before the child died. And see their first-born son . . . alive.

What kind of messed-up crazy world is this?

Noah's parents left the hospital with his death certificate. But no birth certificate. The child died. As a stillborn, the state would not even acknowledge that he ever lived.

My niece and her husband changed that law. After months of due process, in June 2009, the state of Maine passed a new law that required a birth certificate be given to the parents of all stillborn children. It's called "Noah's Law." Stillborn. But born still.[2]

But maybe the state was on to something.

Because isn't that our story? We were born into this crazy-crazy world with a death certificate in hand and no life certificate. At least not the life God originally designed us to have. He wanted us to open our mouths, take our first breath, and breathe His eternal life into our souls. The breath of Eden.

Not the breath of death which steals our children right out of our hands.

What kind of crazy-crazy world is this?

QUESTIONS FOR REFLECTION

What are some ways you now experience the new life in Christ that God created us all to have before the fall—before the start of the universal human condition of spiritual stillbirth?

What is your view of this serpent of old—his power, his ways, his torments?

NOTES

1. Scott C. Todd, *Fast Living: How the Church Will End Extreme Poverty* (Colorado Springs: Compassion International, 2011), 38, 79.

2. To know more about Noah's Law and the ongoing activities of "Noah's Walk," see http://www.noahswalk.com/Certificate_of_Birth.html.

14

BLAME

Reflections on Genesis 3:8–19

*The man said, "The woman whom You gave to be
with me, she gave me from the tree, and I ate."*

—GENESIS 3:12

I made it all about me.

I never sat down and thought it out. I just did it because it was the obvious thing to do. The only thing to do.

It wasn't my fault my mother died. It wasn't my fault my family scattered to the four winds after her funeral. It wasn't my fault I was suddenly living alone in a dormitory in Michigan. Alone. At sixteen. Grieving the loss of my family.

Not my fault.

I raced through the last two years of high school. I raced through college. Near the end of college, I was invited to have dinner with a friend of the family. An older gentleman who had visited my mom in the hospital.

"She knew she was dying," he told me. "She hated that you were so young. She was concerned for you and your older sister and brother."

The more he talked the more I heard what I didn't want to hear.

Not her fault.

I knew it wasn't her fault. She didn't choose cancer. She didn't ask to die at the age of forty-five. I knew that . . . in my head. But my heart was different.

God did this. Mom did this. My dad, my brother, my sister—we had a home. Then we didn't. When it came time to grieve, no one was there. Just me. In a boarding school full of people I didn't know.

Not my fault.

They did three things. One, fig leaves to cover themselves. So she couldn't see him; he couldn't see her. Two, trees to hide behind. So the Lord couldn't see them. And better yet, they couldn't see Him as He came near, the presence of His glory so bright. Three, then came the words. The Lord asked, "Have you eaten from the tree of which I commanded you not to eat?" (Gen. 3:11).

He should have said, "Yes, I did." But he didn't. Instead, he did the unthinkable. Something he'd never have done when the life of God was coursing through his veins. But that life, that eternal God-breathed life was now gone and a new life, a horrible sin-ridden, dark-infested death life was in him.

Not because the fruit was poisonous. It wasn't. The poison came from his own act of disobedience. He did this. He brought this on himself.

But he did the unthinkable. He took out his finger and he used it. He pointed at God and blamed Him: "The woman whom You gave to be with me" (Gen. 3:12). It was *His* fault.

He was the One who made the woman, gave the woman, and knew what the woman was capable of doing to him.

You did this.

Then he pointed at his wife and blamed her saying, "She gave me from the tree, and I ate" (Gen. 3:12).

She did this.

The Eden finger outstretched. Pointing every which way. Blaming the Lord he loved. Blaming the wife he loved. Betraying them both and betraying himself because he blamed them and loved them. How can you do both?

"What is this you have done?" the Lord God said to Eve (Gen. 3:13).

And she should have said, "I ate from the tree You told us not to eat from." But instead, she did what her husband did. She got out her finger and pointed right at the place where she last saw the serpent—who, by now, was long gone—and she said, "The serpent deceived me and I ate" (Gen. 3:13).

The serpent did this.

Not my fault.

It's what we do. It's what sin is all about. It's an all-consuming passion for self-preservation and self-justification, which comes out the moment we're tested. Or when we're guilty of a crime. Or when bad things happen to us. Or when our world turns upside down. The finger comes out. Pointing at everybody and anybody. Past or present. In heaven above or in hell below. Even the ones we love the most. Tossing them under the bus as if we don't care. As if we've never cared.

Self reigning supreme in the kingdom of darkness.

Not my fault.

My heart had to change.

A Christian friend came alongside me in those days and helped me walk through the grief I'd stuffed down so deep inside me. It's a hard process. It always is. And it always starts the same way. Taking my finger pointed at others and turning it to me. To my heart and soul.

I hated seeing my own sin and selfishness. I was so busy blaming everyone for what happened to me that I couldn't see what I was doing. But I was putting self in the center. Always self. Pushing away those I love. Being angry with God.

The Eden finger. Now, finally, pointed at me. Self-centered, sin-filled me.

And the moment that happened, I felt a new freedom come, which allowed me to grieve. I wept for my mom. I wept for all the pain she suffered. I missed her so much.

No more fig leaves. No more hiding behind trees. No more words lashing out against others. It was time to own my own sin. To confess it before the Lord. And to trust Him to help me start a new life in Jesus Christ.

With Him—not me—at the center.

QUESTIONS FOR REFLECTION

Are you good at using your Eden finger—blaming others, blaming God, for all the wrong in your life?

What happens if you put down the Eden finger or, better yet, turn it toward yourself?

15

FEAR

Reflections on Genesis 3:8–24

*He said, "I heard the sound of You in
the garden, and I was afraid."*

—Genesis 3:10

I was eight, and Mom was still alive. It was my first big trip out with her. Every year she took the train from Detroit to Chicago to stay with her aunt and uncle and undergo medical tests. One year she took my brother, the next my sister, and then it was my turn.

Aunt Jo and Uncle Lee lived in a skyscraper, an apartment way up high overlooking the city. It was spectacular at night—everything lit up and everything in motion as far as the eye could see. People, traffic, blinking lights, billboards accompanied by the distant sounds of police sirens and car horns. It felt like there was magic in the air. Like something exciting was just about to burst and explode like fireworks in the evening sky.

For me, at eight years old, it was breathtaking!

And I had my own room. With big windows. Big enough for the lights to pour in and fill every corner of the bedroom.

I dove under my covers happy, like it was Christmas Eve again. My mom, aunt, and uncle all kissed me goodnight.

I fell asleep safe.

But in the middle of the night all that changed. I had a bad dream—the kind I had when I was younger. When I was sick with the flu. When everything is suddenly way out of proportion. Big things become little. Little things become big. My heart would race and suddenly I'd be awake, running to the big city windows of my bedroom.

Looking out. Looking down. Way down.

And I was afraid. More than afraid. It was like fear came alive and jumped on top of me. I put my hands on the window pane in front of me, but it was gone. I felt this hand behind me, pushing me out, and I began to fall, really fall. Down and down. Spinning out of control. The ground coming closer and closer.

My insides convulsed in panic. I was going to die.

We were so high up. I was falling so fast. All I could do was open my mouth and scream as loud as I could. Scream with everything inside me.

Fear. Crazy fear, rushing through every part of my body. Running cold through my veins. Not from some monster lurking in the shadows of the room near me—but here on top of me, here inside me, roaring so loud I thought I was going to hit the ground. I thought I was going to die, and I didn't want to die. I screamed so loud Aunt Jo came rushing into the room first, then Mom and Uncle Lee. They held me until they drove the fear away. They told me I was safe again. Safe from the monster. Safe . . . for now.

But I knew he was still there. They'd never convince me otherwise. I knew it wasn't over. Soon enough, when the time was right, when I was all alone, he'd come back for me.

"I was afraid." It was the first thing Adam said to the Lord after he ate. It was one of the first signs that something was wrong. Majorly wrong. Fear was never intended to be part of the story. It's not how they were made.

Fear has no place in God. Adam and Eve were made perfect in His image. Without sin. Without fear. Without death.

But now fear is alive inside Adam. Real fear. Sin has entered into his body and, because of it, his body has changed. It was never meant to be mortal, even though it was made of dust—a special kind of dust, perfect Paradise dust (Gen. 2:7; see also 3:17).

They were made by God and fit for His eternal life to dwell in their immortal bodies. But "in the twinkling of an eye," they were changed (1 Cor. 15:52). Real, physical change on the inside.

Sin indwelling. Fear, corruption, and death—real death—now inside their mortal dust (Rom. 7:21–33). Then multiply it by the incomprehensible because that change happened on the outside too. Their world changed. The Eden they knew, the Eden they loved, their home, their safe, perfect place where they walked in the light and glory of God.

Banished.

They were driven out of Eden. They were denied access to the Tree of Life. There were no do-overs. No "sorry" and "let's pretend this never happened." No treating their disobedience as a "bad day" and "we'll get past all this."

What He said was true. The Lord God told them that on the day they ate from the Tree of Knowledge of Good and Evil, they would surely die. And they did. They lived physically but died spiritually. They died to the life of God that was in them. They died to God, the author of life Himself (Gen. 2:17; see also Acts. 3:15).

And they were driven out, thrust out of Paradise. Tossed into a terrifying world filled with monsters. Dark, scary, completely unsafe. A world so filled with oppression, wickedness, violence, earthquakes, thunder, famine, and war that no one could escape the ever-present reality that death is always near.

Every day. Every moment of every day.

So that thousands of years later, half the people on the planet live in such extreme poverty they can't find enough to eat, find clean water to drink, provide or protect their children from disease or injustice. All they can do—all we can do—is beg for a paradise big enough to give us the basics to survive today so we might live to see tomorrow.

I got the smallest taste of this at the age of eight.

There I was, a little boy standing at a window in a big skyscraper in Chicago at night. My belly still full from dinner. My heart racing from a bad dream.

I see him. I feel him. I know him. The monster lives. And I do the only thing I know to do.

I scream.

QUESTIONS FOR REFLECTION

What kind of power does fear have in your life?

Have you ever experienced the tangible presence of God in your life so real, so full, that all your fears disappeared and you knew the wonder of Psalm 23:4?

16

SOMEWHERE SAFE

Reflections on Genesis 3:15 and 3:24

*So He drove the man out; and at the east of the garden
of Eden He stationed the cherubim and the flaming sword which
turned every direction to guard the way to the tree of life.*

—Genesis 3:24

The door closed.

Adam and Eve had been expelled from Eden. Far away from the only home they knew. Far away from the only One they loved. In a land of darkness "with devils filled."[1]

To them, it must have felt like hell itself. Anywhere outside the glory of God must feel like hell in comparison. How does anyone live here? Outside the door?

But they weren't in hell. Because hell is where that door shuts forever. It never opens again. Never. And that's not the story here. Adam and Eve were given a promise and they held it tight in their hands. A promise given by God Himself.

One day that door would open again. One day, He promised, a child would come from the woman who would crush the serpent and bring them home. The details were sketchy, but the promise was the promise of God.

And hope was born. One day, one day soon, they'd leave this God-forsaken land and be home again.

She sat at one end of the couch. Her husband next to her. A toddler in her arms. An infant in his. A young child playing at their feet. She was crying. He was crying. Their tears seemed real to me.

He'd been caught.

He messed up. He'd kept his affair secret. No way she'd ever know. But they were out to dinner a few nights back and he stupidly put his phone on the table as a sign of concern. In case the babysitter called.

A text came in.

His wife grabbed the phone faster than him. She thought it had to be from the babysitter. It wasn't. It was a text from another woman who wrote that she missed him. She wanted him. She needed him to call. Now.

She threw the phone at him and demanded an answer.

"I can explain this," he started. But he couldn't, and she bolted from the restaurant. Out to the parking lot. Circling their car, crying.

This wasn't the first time. But back then he made promises. He worked hard to make it up to her. He said it would never happen again, and she believed him. He started going to church. They had their third child. Things were different.

But they weren't different.

Now, sitting on my living room couch, it was like they were in two separate worlds. He was saying all the right things. He talked about God. He talked about getting help, real help. That he was determined to change.

His tears seemed genuine. He said he knew he was on the verge of losing his wife, his children, his home. And it scared him. He didn't want that. "I don't know what else to do," he said pleading.

But for her it was like he wasn't even in the room. She spoke as if he'd already left her. As if he'd packed up his clothes. Grabbed his belongings. Stormed down the stairs without even kissing their children good-bye. The door slamming behind him.

And she was alone. Completely alone. With no idea what to do next. How was she supposed to raise the children by herself? How was she going to provide for them? Put food on the table? Take care of them when they were sick? How was she supposed to get a job and be a mom to her kids?

There was fear in her eyes.

"I'm right here," he said, reaching for her hand. "I'm not going to leave you."

But she knew the story because she knew him. And she was right.

A few weeks later, in the early morning hours, before the kids were up. Before she was up. He made good on one of his promises. He told the woman he loved that he loved her enough to leave his wife. And that's exactly what he did as he slipped down the stairs.

The door closing behind him.

"I don't know what to do," she cried. "I'm afraid for the kids. I'm afraid for me. I don't know how we're going to make it."

In a land of darkness "with devils filled."

But we have a promise given to us by God. He said one day the door would be open again. Back to Eden. Back to Him. He said He'd deal with the problem. He said we'd be welcomed home.

But how does that help now? What are we supposed to do while we wait? Are we abandoned here? Forsaken? Will He help us, protect us, keep us safe?

There was only one way to find out. The men and women of old began to "call upon the name of the LORD" (Gen. 4:26; 12:8). It was both a cry to heaven as well as an act of proclaiming His name. Proclaiming who He is. His nature. His attributes. What He has done. What He has promised. The Lord. Our Maker. Our Hope.[2]

And the Lord heard. And He came. He promised to be with us whenever we'd call on His name. He promised never to fail us or forsake us (Deut. 31:6–8; Josh. 1:5; Heb. 13:5).

It was true then. It's true now.

And it was true for this mom and her three children, as Christians came around her to help, to provide, to pray, to see her through those first weeks and months. She found what we all find when we call upon the Lord.

He is here, just like He promised. In this land of dark and terror. He is here.

And where He is, we find somewhere safe.

QUESTIONS FOR REFLECTION

Too often we find our identity on this side of the door and not on Eden's side where we belong. Does the promise of citizenship in Eden mean anything to you? (See Phil. 3:20.)

Do you know how to call upon the Lord, alone or with others, and find His promise is real?

NOTES

1. Martin Luther's hymn," A Mighty Fortress Is Our God," verse 3.

2. See Acts 2:21 quoted from Joel 2:32. Also, the distinction between calling out to the Lord and the act of proclaiming His name is convincingly argued by Old Testament scholar Allen P. Ross in his book, *Recalling the Hope of Glory: Biblical Worship from the Garden to the New Creation* (Grand Rapids, Mich.: Kregal, 2006), 142–146.

PART 3

CALLING IN JESUS

17
WHO CALLS SO LOUD?

Reflections on Genesis 4:1–17

And the LORD had regard for Abel and for his offering.
—GENESIS 4:4

She was talking . . . smiling. It was a beautiful night. A number of us were out to dinner. She seemed confident, even as tears welled up in her eyes.

It was the last thing she wanted.

She was trying to tell us how right it was to break up with her boyfriend. It didn't work and that was fine with her. She tried to move the conversation along until these stupid tears came out of nowhere. She dabbed the corner of her eyes and apologized. For just a moment, she opened up. She told us she felt burned again. These guys come into her life promising the world—convincing, genuine, the real deal, but they're not. By the time she figures it out, she's been hurt by them. Really hurt.

She painted the story so well. There were too many people in her life telling her what to do, where to go, who to see. She felt pulled in every direction. And nothing seemed to

work. She was tired of it. She wanted things to work out
for her. The right guy. The right job. A heart that felt cared
for and loved. Tears that would go away.

I told her I thought it was something we all want.

How do any of us know what to do? Where to go? Who
to trust? She's right—there are too many voices in this
world calling out to us. Making promises. Showing us the
way to a new Eden if we just do what they say. Go where
they go. Invest ourselves fully. A long, winding, complicated road that, more often than not, leads to a dead end.

Too many voices.

It gets worse. It's here, in heartache and frustration, that
we call out to God. We soon find out there's confusion here
too. Again, too many voices. Everyone has their own view
of God. Everyone wants us to believe what they believe
and worship who they worship. Who's right? What are we
supposed to do? How are we supposed to figure it out?

Why is everything so confusing?

But that's the world we live in. A world called confusion. It's the place Adam and Eve entered after they were
driven out of the real Eden. This place of a thousand voices
calling for us—pulling, enticing, teasing, hurting. Making
us feel so lost.

But it's here, in this confusing world, that we find the story
of Cain and Abel coming to worship God. Cain came with
an offering from his work in the fields. Abel came with an
offering from his work with the flocks. And the Bible says,
"The LORD had regard for Abel and for his offering; but for
Cain and for his offering He had no regard" (Gen. 4:4–5).

This angered Cain.

But the Lord made His appeal to him: "If you do well, will not your countenance be lifted up? And if you do not do well, sin is crouching at the door; and its desire is for you, but you must master it" (Gen. 4:7–8).

The image is terrifying: sin crouching at the door, desiring us. Sin is depicted as something alive, something with passion and feeling. As if it's the Devil himself, prowling around "like a roaring lion, seeking someone to devour" (1 Pet. 5:8). Calling us. Wooing us. Wanting us.

The moment we bend our ear in his direction, the sound of all the voices grows louder. It's simply true: The Devil knows how to make his appeal to us. Lure us. Excite us. Tempt us. Deceive us. He knows how to appeal to our sinful, fallen nature. He knows how to make promises that offer everything we want. He knows how to make his one voice into a thousand voices so that our lives are a constant running after disappearing dreams.

His voice is strong and persuasive, loud and demanding. More times than not, he mimics the voice of God. Salted with words from Scripture. Clothed as an "angel of light" (2 Cor. 11:14). Confusing us about who God is, what God has said, what God has done more than we could ever imagine.

It's the voice Cain followed.

But that's not Abel's story.

And this is our hope. In a world of a thousand voices, one voice stands above them all. From the very beginning of time, as we entered this dark, terrifying world called confusion, we have something that is sure. Trustworthy.

God speaks. His word is true. We can trust it. We can trust Him.

This is the wonderful, powerful witness of Scripture. In Hebrews 11:4, we are told that Abel came to God by faith. What does this mean? It means that God called to Him. He spoke to Him. He opened Abel's heart to hear and believe Him. He gave the gift of faith—faith that believes—faith that "comes from hearing" (Rom. 10:17).

And Abel responded. Cain did not. Cain turned away. But Abel came in obedience with the offering God required. He did what was right because he knew what was right, because he knew the voice of the One he loved.

One voice above all the rest. One voice calling us by name. One voice calling us to come, follow Him, and say no to the other voices crouching at the door and say yes to Him.

But can we hear Him who calls so loud? Can we hear and respond to the only voice that matters?

QUESTIONS FOR REFLECTION

In John 10, Jesus said that His own know His voice. It's simple, not hard. Is it simple for you? Or are you lost in a world of too many voices?

It's hard to break from the crowd. It cost Abel his life to do what was right. Are you able to hear Him and do what He calls you to do?

18

YOU'RE KIDDING, RIGHT?

Reflections on Genesis 6

But Noah found favor in the eyes of the LORD.

—GENESIS 6:8

My friend broke from the crowd.

"I didn't take it," he told me. We were at a church picnic in Pittsburgh. My friend had been offered a promotion of a lifetime. "It's hard for Mary and me," he went on. "We need the money. We've had a hard time financially these past years and this would make a huge difference in our lives."

"So why turn it down?" I butted in.

"At first we didn't want to. But the more we prayed and talked, the more we realized the Lord wants us to raise our kids—and do it well. If I take this job, I'll be working late every night and gone a couple weekends a month. It means travel. Time away from my family. We don't believe the Lord wants that for our children."

"So you've already said no?"

"Yeah, my boss was really surprised. I'm sure he thinks I'm crazy. He tried to talk me into it, but it didn't work.

I know what the Lord has called us to do and that's all that matters."

I wanted to say, "You're kidding, right?" He was in his mid-thirties, hardworking, conscientious—at the perfect time for promotion. Most Christians I know wouldn't have given it a second thought. They'd tell me, "The Lord has done this! His name be praised!"

Not him. He broke from the crowd. They both did. Who turns down promotions? Who says no to more money for the sake of family and children?

I saw such strength and resolve in my friend that day. I saw faith as clear as I'd ever seen it.

But faith on a deeper level. I'd always thought faith was a gift given by God to the heart and soul of someone who didn't know Him. Faith that opens our eyes to see, know, and believe that Jesus is the Christ, the Son of God, who has come from the Father to rescue us. "And without faith it is impossible to please Him, for he who comes to God must believe that He is and that He is a rewarder of those who seek Him" (Heb. 11:6).

That's what I thought. It's about people coming to faith.

It belongs to that company of people who have heard Him call them by name. And in hearing, this gift of faith fills the heart and comes with the power to turn away from the stuff of evil in their lives and to turn to Him. Go to Him. Follow Him and become His, once and forever.

But I saw something different in my friend, something deeper. He had more than saving faith. He had faith to obey God.

I thought back on the early days of the Bible. Back at the beginning, when our forebears were exiled from Eden, and the world soon became a place where evil and wickedness reigned. Wickedness beyond imagining as the whole earth became "corrupt" and "filled with violence" (Gen. 6:11–13). The masses of people were soon bent on thinking and doing "evil continually" (Gen. 6:5). And one man stood out. One man broke from the crowd.

He heard the Lord call him by name. He had faith to believe. This is what I thought the Bible meant in Hebrews 11:7 when it says, "By faith Noah . . ." It meant Noah was given the gift to believe, and in believing he "found favor in the eyes of the LORD" (Gen. 6:8).

Favor to believe. Yes, but more.

He had favor to do what the Lord was calling him to do. "Noah was a righteous man, blameless in his time; Noah walked with God" (Gen. 6:9). He didn't do what the people of his time were doing. He didn't follow in the way of evil and corruption. What powerful words: He walked with God! He heard Him call. He received faith—saving faith.

But more. He had faith to say yes to God.

And that faith grew. Soon enough the Lord gave Noah eyes to see what was about to happen. Judgment was about to come on the whole earth. Judgment that would fore-shadow the great day of judgment at the end of time and would, like the destruction of Sodom and Gomorrah, be an "example to those who would live ungodly lives thereafter" (2 Pet. 2:5–6). It would, for every generation, be a picture of the wrath of God against the wickedness of man. Noah knew it. He saw it before it happened.

And that's when the Lord told him to build an ark.

You're kidding, right?

The world around us calls this kind of faith crazy, hyper-religious fanaticism. But down through the ages, there has always been a company of people like Noah, like my Pittsburgh friend, who want to live by faith. They want to do only what God is calling them to do.

It's not saving faith. It's deeper than that. It's obedient faith. Faith given at a specific time for a specific task for a specific reason. Faith that shows how to take the next step, break from the crowd if we have to, and go for the prize God has for us.

I want that obedient faith in my life. That crazy faith that wouldn't mind telling people, as Noah did, "Hey, guess what? We're building an ark!" And they might ask, "Why are you doing that?" Noah might say back, "Because the Lord has called me to and I said yes."

You're kidding, right?

I want to go deeper. I want to ask Him for obedient faith. Faith that steps out and does what He's calling me to do. Faith like my friend had. I know it cost him and his family to turn down that promotion. I know it always comes with cost. But I want the courage, strength, and power that comes with saying yes to Him even as the world around me mockingly laughs in surprise.

You're kidding, right?

QUESTIONS FOR REFLECTION

Are there people in your life who model this obedient faith, who show the courage to do what is right?

Is there something today you need to say no to in order to say yes to what the Lord wants from you?

19

WHEN US COMES DOWN

Reflections on Genesis 11:1–9

*They said, "Come, let us build for ourselves a city,
and a tower whose top will reach into heaven,
and let us make for ourselves a name."*

—GENESIS 11:4

Rebellion can be so cultured, found in the jealous pursuit of high society.

I met this man once. He was making a name for himself. He went to the right schools. He got the right positions in good companies. He marched up the career ladder. He even broke the pattern and launched his own company to the admiration of his colleagues.

This man lived in the right house in the right part of town. He had a good family with the kids in the right schools. His friends were all in the same strata of society, each quietly competing to build their kingdoms a little bigger, a little higher than the others. Just enough for people to admire. And dream, wishing they could be like them.

I remember this guy talking to my dad. His said his goal in life was simple. He wanted to make a name greater than his father's. He didn't. But he spent his life trying.

I was fourteen. My dad told me that life was more than making a name for myself. I was so proud of my parents. They always put family first even though they fit into this society: Dad in his work; Mom in her charity work in town. We went to the right church. We belonged to the right organizations. Socialized in the right places with the right people.

Everything was perfect.

Until one day, it wasn't. It all came down. In hindsight, it was the perfect storm. Dad's business lost its footing in an economic recession. Mom's health took a turn. We'd later find out it was cancer. Inoperable cancer. Dad was being transferred to California, then to London. My older brother and sister were in college and working. My mom, five months after her diagnosis, died.

It was gone. All of it.

I didn't know it then. But I'd just witnessed the first principles of this broken, fallen life. It was like I'd walked into the engine room of the universe and saw firsthand what makes the world go round. It's so simple, so clear. It's what drives us.

The pursuit up.

Later I learned this principle was in the Bible. The prophets tell us that the Devil himself, before he fell from glory, experienced this first evil passion: "But you said in your heart, 'I will ascend to heaven; I will raise my throne above the stars of God, and I will sit on the mount of assembly in the recesses of the north. I will ascend above the heights of the clouds; I will make myself like the Most High'" (Isa. 14:13–14).[1]

The pursuit up.

I saw it all around me. I saw it in me. Cloaked in the deceptive argument that I was pursuing excellence, I found instead that I was pursuing up. Striving for acceptance. Driving for bigger, better, more—so others could see. As if what I witnessed in my family at fourteen never happened. Or better yet, wouldn't happen to me.

You'd think I'd learn. You'd think we'd all learn.

You'd think after Noah's flood, when the Lord brought judgment on the world for sin, for turning to our own way and not His, that all generations from that point on would learn the lesson. We'd stop and remember, learn and choose the better way. But we didn't. We don't.

We keep repeating. Over and over. The pursuit up.

This is what the Bible says. It's what the Lord wants us to see and understand. But the generations after Noah forgot the past and devoted themselves to the pursuit up. They built a tower into the heavens. Why? To make a name for themselves.

They said, "Come, let us build for ourselves a city, and a tower whose top will reach into heaven, and let us make for ourselves a name, otherwise we will be scattered abroad over the face of the whole earth" (Gen. 11:4).

The passion of the Devil has become the passion of our hearts. To ascend. To build our kingdoms. To establish our empires. To reach the heavens. To exalt our name. Not His— ours. Here's the ultimate rebellion: to reject God, to promote self. To make a world where we're at the top. Sitting in His seat.

It's called the Tower of Babel. It belongs both to our past and to our future. The Bible ends with the world becoming the city of Babylon. Like this story, and this principle, it never goes away. It only increases and intensifies.

The pursuit up.

Can't you see it all around you? In people, in ourselves, in small business, in big business, in mergers and takeovers, in nations warring against nations? Isn't this the cause of our quarrels and divisions? Our jealousies and hatred? Can't you see it even in our churches? Among our Christians?

It permeates everything. Always has. Always will. Until that moment comes, and it always comes, when the Lord Himself steps in. "Come, let Us go down" (Gen. 11:7).

And that's what He does. He comes down. The eternal Us—Father, Son, and Holy Spirit. He ends the day of our rebellion. He tears down our kingdoms and empires. He puts an end to the evil passion of pursuing up.

Until it's gone. All of it. Everything we've built in our name, for our name. Because that principle is not in Him. It's not His kingdom. It's not who He is or what He does. When will we learn that?

When will we learn not to pursue up but to pursue Him and His glory? Because we must, before it's too late. Before it happens.

When Us comes down.

QUESTIONS FOR REFLECTION

Can you find the principle in you, this pursuit up?

How is life different if our passions and pursuits are for His glory and His name, not our own?

NOTE

1. See Ezekiel 28:11–19 as a prophetic reference to Satan's downfall.

20

BUT WHEN GOD CALLS

~~~

Reflections on Genesis 12:1–3

Go forth from your country, and from your relatives and
from your father's house, to the land which I will show you.

—GENESIS 12:1

He had no idea it was his last Sunday in the pulpit. After thirty years as the pastor of the church, this was it.

He didn't feel well. But he thought it was just the lingering effects of the flu he couldn't shake. But it didn't stop him from preaching that Sunday. It was February 25, 1968.

For fifty-six weeks, he had been preaching on John 4. On this particular Sunday, his message was strong. He emphasized that the miraculous work of God in the soul of the Christian changes what we are. At our core.

"We have been emphasizing the importance of what we are. We are bound to start here because what we are is altogether more significant than what we do."[1]

The heartache is this: We put on the image.

"Very many people give the impression of having inward peace and tranquility when everything is going well . . . and the sun is shining in the heavens. . . . But the test comes when everything goes wrong. . . . This is one of the most profound tests that we can ever apply to ourselves."[2]

The tests come, he thundered. But for the Christian, there is this inner peace in the midst of the test, an inner resource we can depend on. "And so the more adverse and cruel and trying the circumstances . . . the more it drives you to realize that you do not belong to this world, that you are bigger than it, that you belong to Christ. You belong to heaven, you belong to glory—a far more exceeding and eternal weight of glory . . . independent of circumstances."[3]

He gave the example of the apostle Paul, bound in chains, pleading with King Agrippa, and saying in effect, "I would give anything if only you people could be as I am. Oh, I wish you had the inner peace and the rest that I am enjoying!" (See Acts 26:27–29.)

"Here is a man who is entirely independent of his circumstances—they make no difference to him. He has inner reserves . . . given through the Lord Jesus Christ by the Holy Spirit."[4]

This, he said, is the wonder of being a Christian. We can face whatever comes our way in Christ. And it is this that makes our witness strong to the world.

No matter what comes our way.

The next Sunday morning at 8:00 a.m. his wife called the assistant pastor. The matter was urgent. He needed to race to church and preach for her husband who was suffering from abdominal pains. Later that week, her husband was admitted to the hospital and underwent major surgery where cancer was discovered.

In the weeks that followed, as the preacher recovered, he and his wife knew that his days in the pastorate were over. As difficult as it was, they both knew the Lord had stepped in and issued a new call on their lives. In his testimony to others, he'd write: "But when God calls, He is to be obeyed in spite of all natural feelings."[5]

I love these words: But when God calls. I marvel at stories like this. This Christian preacher had no idea the trials that were soon coming upon him and yet there he was, in the pulpit the week before, describing the wonder of what Jesus Christ does inside us—in making us His very own—able to face any circumstance.

And then, in a few days' time, he was put to the test.

The Lord was profoundly at work in his life, calling him in a new direction. A scary direction. Cancer. The end of his pastorate. The unknown.

But that's the way it is with the Lord. He calls. He makes a certain part of His will known to us. I wish sometimes He'd make it all known to us. And, when He does, that it would come with bolts of lightning. Peals of thunder. His voice really, really clear so we can't miss it.

Like He did with the great patriarch, Abraham. "The God of glory appeared to our father Abraham . . . and said to him, 'Leave your country'" (Acts 7:2–3).

This is so direct. The Lord dynamically revealed His glory, His will, His purpose to Abraham. But no matter how He reveals Himself to us and calls us, only one thing is necessary. We must hear Him, and in hearing, by faith, respond. "By faith Abraham, when he was called, obeyed by going out to a place which he was to receive for an inheritance; and he went out, not knowing where he was going" (Heb. 11:8).

Abraham went out. Not knowing.

Like that preacher in 1968, stepping out into the unknown. Completely unsure of what the next step might be.

But here's the secret. We know the One calling. So it doesn't matter what the circumstances are. It only matters that He is with us, leading us. That He is doing a work in us. A profound work, at our core. Giving us that inner peace in Christ that comes only by being made pure, made to be holy—this is a peace that makes what we are infinitely more significant than what we do. And at the end of the day, knowing God is more significant than life itself.

That preacher lived another thirteen years, serving the Lord until the day he died. And the witness he gave at this crucial moment in his life always strengthens and challenges me.

To be ready in the day of testing. To be listening.

But when God calls!

QUESTIONS FOR REFLECTION

Do you believe that if our identity is rooted in the One who we know, not in what we do, we can face the unknown?

Can you look back and see, hear, and know God's calling on your life? What about now?

NOTES

1. Martyn Lloyd-Jones, *Living Water: Studies in John 4* (Wheaton, Ill.: Crossway, 2009), 716.

2. Ibid., 720.

3. Ibid., 725–726.

4. Ibid., 723.

5. Iain H. Murray, *David Martyn Lloyd-Jones: The Fight of Faith 1939–1981* (Carlisle, Pa.: Banner of Truth, 1990), 588.

21

BAGGAGE

Reflections on Genesis 12:4–20

*So Abram went forth as the LORD had spoken
to him; and Lot went with him.*

—GENESIS 12:4

Do you remember Linus and his blanket, from the old *Peanuts* comic strip? Hard to believe something so simple, so darn cute, can reveal so much about me.

I say it all the time, "Everything's fine!" (as long as I have my blanket, or actually, blankets).

Definitely two kinds of blankets. Those I know about and those I don't. The ones I know about, those absolute necessities in my life (which really aren't but I think they are), tend to be the leading edge of the Lord's dealings with me.

But the ones I don't know about actually scare me more. Call it culture. Or upbringing. Or the sinful nature. But I rely on a ton of stuff I'm blind to.

I call it baggage. Lots and lots of baggage.

When I think about this, I remember Abraham's story. The Lord, the God of glory, appeared to Abraham and told him, "Go forth from your country, and from your relatives and from your father's house, to the land which I will show you" (Gen. 12:1). And he did. He obeyed and by faith "went out, not knowing where he was going" (Heb. 11:8).

Yeah, but . . . he took his dad. The Lord said to leave his relatives behind. Most likely this was a cultural moment, a culture that put father in a position of authority. And though they set out under the Lord's command "in order to enter the land of Canaan," they took a little detour and settled in the city of Haran (Gen. 11:31). Until his dad died. It was then that Abraham resumed his course to Canaan.

The Bible states the facts of the story without commentary. But it's not hard to understand. Our obedience to the Lord often comes with a ton of baggage. Baggage that we may be blind to. We're so used to our culture that we hear the Lord through the filters of what we know.

The Lord says, "Leave your relatives." But the ears hear, "He's not talking about Dad." So, from our perspective, there's no sense of disobedience. No inkling of rebellion or an impure heart. It actually feels like 100 percent obedience.

And then there's his nephew, Lot. He takes him too.

And then there's a famine once Abraham arrives in the Promised Land. You'd think he'd turn to the Lord, seek His counsel, and ask Him what to do. But no. Instead, he relied on his natural instincts and headed off for Egypt where there was food (Gen. 12:10).

Baggage. Tons and tons of baggage.

Of course, in crises, we resort to what we know, what we've done in the past, how we think, how we normally handle life issues. It's there in Egypt where he felt his life threatened. His wife, even at her age, was gorgeous. Desirable. Abraham feared that Pharaoh would want her and kill him to get her.

So he lied. Or, maybe, half-lied.

Why did he do that? Because the culture allowed it. Because, even now, we know that cultural white lies are permissible for self-protection. Isn't that right? Isn't it reasonable?

Baggage. Tons and tons of baggage.

And then there's the story of the woman they picked up in Egypt named Hagar. It doesn't seem like a problem at first. It's normal to the culture so Abraham had no need to go to the Lord and seek His counsel. This too becomes a problem later.

There's no question about it. Abraham obeyed the Lord. By faith, he did what he understood to do. But we can see in this story one simple fact: Abraham was not perfect. Abraham's obedience was muddled with the sins of the flesh and the times.

Just like us.

But the good news is that he grew; he matured in faith and obedience. This is the same man who, later in life, would obey to such an extent as to offer his promised son back to the Lord (Gen. 22).

Doesn't that give us amazing hope?

But the process isn't always easy. The more we walk with the Lord, the more He gives us eyes to see the baggage we're blind to. Blankets we've long trusted.

Blankets I still clutch. That I don't want taken from me. Blankets that make me feel secure. Simple things. The way I think. The way I act. How I make decisions. How I handle tough situations. I rely on what I know. I fall back on what's worked in the past. I turn to others who have common sense. Business sense. People sense. Years of schooling. Years of experience. A gut feeling. A good reputation.

Why don't I turn to the Lord first? To my brothers and sisters in Christ to pray and seek good and godly counsel?

But too often I don't. I rely on my own strength. Especially in times of crisis.

I can feel it deep in my soul, especially when I've gone to developing countires. When it feels like every security blanket I've ever known is taken away from me and I'm left to trust the Lord. Just Him and Him alone.

With no sense that the locks on the doors are secure. No phone next to the bed. No 911 to call if rebels suddenly come out of the bush and storm the compound. No hospital nearby that will take care of us if we survive. No sense that justice will reign, always reign, if the world turns upside down.

No place called safe. Here in this world, I saw thousands of Christian people living in the heart of unimaginable poverty. Yet there they are, trusting the Lord to be their safety—the only blanket they need. They know what I long to know—where He is, there is safety.

Even when sickness comes—and rebels come—and death comes.

Baggage. I've got tons and tons of baggage.

QUESTIONS FOR REFLECTION

What do you know about your blankets, seen and unseen?

It's hard when blankets go. I find sometimes my identity gets shaken—I needed those blankets to be me. Is it the same for you?

22

HE MAKES HELL LOOK LIKE EDEN

Reflections on Genesis 13:1–13

Abram settled in the land of Canaan, while Lot settled in the cities of the valley, and moved his tents as far as Sodom.

—Genesis 13:12–13

It was like I could see it. This power coming through the open windows. As if a giant magnet was just outside on the street, grabbing us. Demanding us.

I was preaching at the local rescue mission at the Wednesday morning chapel. There was a sense of grief in the room. A staff member, one of the graduates of the year-long Christian discipleship program for drug and alcohol addiction, was gone.

Back on the street. They call it "relapse."

He had been doing so well. He had stayed at the mission as a worker, friend, mentor, and encourager to those newly off the streets.

And he was gone.

I stood at the lectern. The windows were behind me. One to my left. One to my right. It was then that I could feel this power coming through the windows. Seductive power preaching its own gospel message: "Come back to the streets. You can handle it now. The God talk is all a lie. It can never satisfy you. Never!"

It's so hard to understand. How is it possible to paint life on the streets as attractive, desirable, a longing of body, soul, and mind that can only be satisfied there? But it is possible. Just stand with those who know the streets and you'll find out. This is their story.

It's a constant battle.

Wear the right glasses, see through the right lens, and suddenly the streets become beautiful. Crazy enticing. Like Paradise beckoning her children home.

This is one of the first principles the Lord teaches in the Bible. It's how He disciples us. He wants us to know the real stuff of life and, specifically, these seductive powers, so we might know how to handle them, how to see with His eyes and deal with them.

For this reason, I go back to the story of Lot.

It was time for Abraham and Lot to have more space between them. There was already strife between their herdsmen, so Abraham gave Lot the choice, and Lot saw the beauty of the Jordan valley. So green and lush and beautiful. Near Sodom.

To him it looked like Eden, "like the garden of the LORD." So Lot "moved his tents as far as Sodom." The Bible says it so simply: "Now the men of Sodom were wicked exceedingly and sinners against the LORD" (Gen. 13:10–13).

Like that power stretching through the rescue mission windows, Lot was caught. At first, he lived near Sodom.

Next thing we know, "he was living in Sodom" (Gen. 14:12). And then, soon enough, he sat at the gates of Sodom as one of the elders of the city (Gen. 19:1).

Enticing, seductive power.

The Bible later tells us that Lot "felt his righteous soul tormented day after day by their lawless deeds" (2 Pet. 2:8). It took a different kind of power, two angels who had to do some serious pushing to get Lot, his wife, and two daughters out of Sodom. And even then, Lot's wife "relapsed." For the last time (Gen. 19:26).

Do we get this?

This is how the Devil works. Always has, always will—until the coming of our Lord. He makes hell look like Eden. If he can make Sodom look like Paradise or the streets full of prostitution and drugs look like hope and opportunity, then he can entice us all back into the sins we know so well.

And make them look perfect. Eden perfect.

The Devil never stops. He's the world power, the magnet, tormenting us to make decisions that look good, feel right, and promise to satisfy our deepest needs. He will do anything and everything to lure us back. To make us make choices contrary to the purpose, plan, and call of God on our lives.

Until we're near Sodom. Then in Sodom. Then tormented by Sodom.

But no, not us. We tend to underestimate the power of the Devil in our lives. We tend to overestimate our ability to handle the sins, lusts, and temptations that come our way. We tend to never estimate that the Devil comes at us—more often than not—in sheep's clothing. Dressed as an "angel of light" (2 Cor. 11:14; see also Matt. 7:15). Urging us to live like the culture. Play like the culture. Worship the gods of the culture.

But dressed as something God-blessed, God-given. And behind that dress is power. Power that commands our attention. Power that appeals to the lusts of our eyes, our flesh, our mind. Power forcing us to choose whether we will turn to the Lord, seek His counsel, and go His way—or yield to the world's power.

That's the story of Lot in Sodom.

At the rescue mission, the pull from the streets is constant. If we thought about it, the same is true for each of us. We know the power of sin, the world, the flesh, and the Devil in our own lives, don't we? It may not come in the form of addiction to drugs or alcohol, but still it comes and in the form we know best.

Power through the windows. Enticing, seductive power.

The Lord wants to disciple us in these things. To know how to see through the Devil's disguises and have the strength in His Holy Spirit to resist, say no, and to live in the freedom given to us in Christ Jesus. This is His gift to us.

But first things first—we need to know something about the Devil's ways.

Be aware. Be on your guard, for he makes hell look like Eden.

QUESTIONS FOR REFLECTION

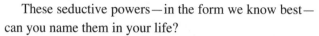

These seductive powers—in the form we know best—can you name them in your life?

These men at the rescue mission always teach me that we need Jesus every day. And I wonder, what makes us think we can handle life on our own?

23

THEN COMES THE BLESSING

~*∂~

Reflections on Genesis 14:17–24

And Melchizedek king of Salem brought out bread and wine;
now he was a priest of God Most High. He blessed him
and said, "Blessed be Abram of God Most High,
Possessor of heaven and earth."

—GENESIS 14:18–19

My friend, Mark Hood, was on the plane that went down in the Hudson River in January 2009. Later that year, I invited him to come to church in Connecticut and tell his story.[1]

He was headed from New York to Charlotte. He's an ex-marine who served his country in the Gulf War and was nearly killed in battle on several occasions. Hard to believe, he told us, that after years in combat he was about to die because a bunch of geese hit the engines. Both engines were gone. Both on fire. The plane was headed into the ice-cold Hudson.

Mark said he grabbed the hands of the woman seated next to him. He told her it was time to pray in Jesus' name. And that's exactly what he did. He began to pray.

As he told this part of the story at our church, something extraordinary happened. A young woman sat enthralled at Mark's every word. Somehow Mark's story was her story. Both out of control, plummeting toward death. And when

Mark grabbed the hands of the woman seated next to him on the plane, it was as if he had grabbed hers too.

She was in need too.

She needed Mark's prayer to be her prayer. She needed Jesus. She needed Him to come and rescue her before everything in her life came crashing down.

And, miracle of miracles, it happened. She'd tell her story a year later as she spoke in front of a crowd of five hundred people. She talked openly of her teenage years lost in drugs. She told us how her dealer had killed other girls and swore he'd kill her if she ever left him.

But she did. She escaped. An older Christian woman found her, took her in, and drove her to a place for treatment out of state. Far enough away so her dealer would never find her. Safe in the arms of Christian people who cared for her and loved her.

Religion, she told the crowd, had never worked for her. She wanted no part of it. But having people love her and be concerned for her every day? Well, that—for the first time—felt good.

Going to church on Sundays, as part of the rehab program, didn't thrill her. But she took it in stride. Until, that is, she came to our church that Sunday Mark Hood came into town, stood in the pulpit, and told his story.

A plane about to crash. Hands reaching over, grabbing hers. The words so clear: It's time to pray in Jesus' name.

I don't know how it happens. I just know that it does. At some point, the Lord steps in and meets with us. Somehow the hands holding ours become His hands and we are suddenly aware the Lord is here with us. He's dealing with us. He's rescuing us.

He's blessing us.

"Jesus Christ came into my life that Sunday morning," she told the crowd. "And my life is not—and will never be—the same because of it."

I marvel at her testimony. I marvel at the woman of God she is becoming all these years later. Behind her story, buried deep beneath her words, are principles the Lord gives us in Scripture. This is what He does. He calls us. He reveals Himself to us. And then, with amazing kindness and love, He blesses us.

This is what happened the day Abraham met Melchizedek.

Abraham knew the Lord. He'd known the call of God in his life and responded in obedience. He'd left his native country. He'd followed Him to the Promised Land. He'd built an altar and there, in the midst of a pagan people worshiping a host of gods, Abraham publically worshiped the Lord, the one true God.

In his compassion, when his nephew Lot had been captured by enemy forces, Abraham went out in battle and rescued him. When the war was over, Melchizedek appeared. He was both king of Salem and priest of God Most High. He came to Abraham to bless him and share a meal of bread and wine.

The Bible tells us that Melchizedek is a type of the Son of God to come (Heb. 7:1–4). Although a real, historical person, he becomes a picture of Jesus Himself meeting Abraham—then having the meal of Communion, bread and wine, with Abraham. And then, the sacred moment, he blessed Abraham.

This blessing from Melchizedek—the blessing of God Himself—becomes everything in Scripture. Abraham takes it and passes it on to his son Isaac. Isaac to Jacob and on through the generations.

This is what the Lord does.

It's who He is. It's how He deals with us. At some point, this story has to be our story. The Lord meets with us. The Lord blesses us. It's sad to say, but we can be in church, be around Christians, and study the Bible all our lives and not know this meeting with Him, this blessing. We can call ourselves Christians and do our best to live as Christians live but never experience this grace He wants to give.

At some point, it has to happen. We have to feel His hands grabbing ours. We have to know—and know for certain—He's here with us. Here, as the plane goes down into the Hudson. Here, when we feel like our life is about to crash and burn. Here, when we call out in the depth of our need and pray in Jesus' name.

We need Him to meet with us. To draw us close. To rescue us. And then to do what He promises to do.

Let the blessing come, and receive it willingly, thankfully.

For when it does, our lives will never be the same.

QUESTIONS FOR REFLECTION

We are a people of story. We are those who have met with Him. Have you met with Him? Has He met with you and blessed you?

Too often, this kind of blessing is seen as physical (prayers being answered) rather than relational (being in communion with Him). Are you wanting to deepen this relationship with Him? Will you pray, "Lord, make this blessing real in my life every day"?

NOTE

1. For more on Mark Hood, see Mark Hood, "Soldier of Faith," in Dorothy Firman and Kevin Quirk, *Stories of Near Death and Hope for New Life* (Deerfield Beach, Fla.: Health Communications, Inc., 2009), 82–89.

24

WITH THE CALL COMES FAITH

Reflections on Genesis 15:1–6

*Then he believed in the LORD; and He reckoned
it to him as righteousness.*

—GENESIS 15:6

I think about Julie a lot.

It was the first church I served as pastor. She was adored by everyone. For over a decade, people came around her to drive her, three times a week, to the dialysis center. When she suffered a heart attack, we were amazed to hear her story.

"I was there," she told us, "in the presence of Jesus!" Then—*thump!*—she was back, looking into the face of a doctor. "Oh, how that surprised me!"

Years later the phone call came. Julie had been taken to the ER. I rushed to the hospital and found her already in the ICU. She was conscious but weak. A team of doctors came in and out until they finally decided to take her to surgery. They wanted her to face another demanding, invasive, altogether risky surgery.

"I'm done," she told them. "I can't do it." She was bleeding internally, just weeks after open heart surgery. The doctors wanted to go in, find it, and stop it. But she didn't have the strength. Her body was done and she knew it.

I will never forget the brightness in her eyes.

Her daughter and I stood on either side of her bed. At some point, Julie asked me to recite Psalm 23. I didn't have my Bible, nor did I have it memorized, so I gave it a try and completely messed it up. Julie looked me straight in the eyes and frowned, "That's not it! You should probably know it by heart," she said, and I nodded, as she poked fun at me.

But what surprised me most was something I'd never seen before. She had faith to go home. Not just faith in the Lord. She had that. I had that. This was different. She had strength in her broken, weak heart to see the door of the kingdom of God opening to her. I saw it as she comforted her daughter. I heard it in the gentleness of her voice. I felt it in the touch of her hand.

Nearing midnight she said to me quietly, "I'm sorry it's taking so long. You need to go home and get rest." And then she smiled. How was it possible? Here she was facing death and she was concerned for me! So peaceful. So ready to go home.

"Julie, I'd rather you not go," I whispered.

But she did. As if it was all perfectly orchestrated, Julie's daughter began to sing "Amazing Grace" and, just before the last verse, the Lord came for Julie. The door opened and she was home at last.

In the weeks and months that followed, I struggled with what happened that night. Julie had faith to die that I didn't have. But why didn't I have it? Shouldn't all Christians have it? I mean, it's the very heart and soul of who we are and what we believe. Jesus Christ has risen from the dead. He has forever defeated death by what He did on Calvary's hill.

Julie knew that. But it was more than just knowing it in her head. She experienced it. She held this faith in her heart, or was held by it, like a little girl safe in the arms of her Father. She was not afraid. But I was. She was not anxious. So why was I?

Does that mean I'm a Christian in my head but not in my heart?

I turned to the Bible. I continued the story God laid out from the beginning. It encouraged me to find that Abraham had the same struggle of faith. This man knew the call of God on his life. He eventually left everything and followed the Lord to the Promised Land. He even received the blessing of Melchizedek.

But he didn't understand.

He was told he was going to have a son. He was an old man. His wife beyond child-bearing years. It was impossible for them to have children. So Abraham did what most of us would do: He came up with his own plan. He reasoned that Eliezer of Damascus, the chief servant born in his house, would be his promised son.

"This man," the Lord shot back, "will not be your heir; but one who will come forth from your own body, he shall be your heir." Then the Lord showed Abraham the stars in the heavens. "Count the stars, if you are able to count them," the Lord declared. "So shall your descendants be" (Gen. 15:4–5).

Then it happened. The impossible became possible. I call it the Genesis 15:6 miracle. The Lord opened Abraham's heart to believe the promise. He gave him the gift of faith to see the child before the child was ever born. This is faith leaping beyond reason! Faith that sees with God's eyes. Faith that knows it's true in the head. Faith that experiences it in the heart. Faith that holds the promise to come as if the promise is already here, held firm in our hands.

This is the gift of God come down from heaven!

Oh, thank God, it's something He does and not something I do. Faith is not something worked up by me or in my own strength. I need to seek it, ask for it, and receive it when it comes. But I can't make it happen. He does that. He opens the heart. He gives the gift to believe in Him. To believe in His promises, and to see what our physical eyes can't see.

That's what Abraham had. Faith to believe in God, yes. But also this special, particular faith to believe that he, in his old age, would have a promised son.

It's also what Julie had.

Julie had a call of God on her life that I didn't have. It was as if she stood at the Jordan River ready to make the crossing into the Promised Land. It was her time. The Lord was calling her home. And with the call came the faith she needed to see Jesus, to know, rejoice, and cross over.

And she did. And I got to be there. At first, it confused me. It made me question everything. But then I understood. The gift the Lord gave me was to have a front-row seat to see her make the crossing. I got to come right up to the banks of the Jordan. I got to see Julie hear the call of God and then to receive the gift of faith that triumphs in the face of death.

The impossible altogether possible.

Faith to go home! I knew that night that someday in the future the same would happen to me. I'll find myself at the riverbank. I'll hear the Lord Jesus Christ call my name. And suddenly my eyes will see. My heart will know. This gift of God will come at just the right time. It's all because of this simple biblical truth I saw lived out in Julie's life that night.

Something I will never forget.

With the call comes faith.

QUESTIONS FOR REFLECTION

There are days I know what God has called me to do, but I don't have the faith for it. Do you know days like that?

I soon learned I could ask Him for faith. If He has called me to serve in a particular way, then He promises with the call comes the faith. Has He done that for you in the past? Do you think He will do it today for you?

PART 4

COVENANT
IN JESUS

25

ONE THING, ONE THING ONLY

Reflections on Genesis 15:7–21

On that day the LORD made a covenant with Abram.

—GENESIS 15:18

What if we have the question wrong?

What if, at the day of judgment, it's not about performance? Not about what we accomplished, the very thing that fills the obituary pages. The very thing most of us have known since childhood: do well, get loved. Same in our adult years: perform well, get paid, get promoted, get motivated to work harder.

So who we are is what we do. And what we do is who we are.

What if the question is about relationships? About people? The very thing the Bible is all about. First, our relationship with God. Next, our relationships with each other.

A man in the Midwest came home one night to his wife. A hard day's work. He hates what he does. Too many years, too many problems. His kids are grown and married with kids of their own. He's counting the years, the months, the days until his retirement. If he could, he'd quit. But he can't. He needs the money and no job pays like this job. Not for what he needs. He's trapped and he knows it.

His wife has news.

She's been diagnosed with stage 4 cancer. They both saw the symptoms and for a while didn't talk about it. Eventually, she talked to her doctor and that began a battery of tests. And this was it, the news they didn't want to hear.

It's going to get worse. They both knew that. It's going to require care. A lot of care. She could have a couple of years at most. But there's no cure. The disease is fatal. They both knew exactly what this diagnosis meant.

A few days passed. Maybe a week.

Her husband went to the attic, pulled down a couple of suitcases, and packed up his clothes. He found some boxes in the garage and filled them with what he needed. Then he loaded up his car and without so much as a good-bye or an explanation as to where he was going or how long he'd be gone. He drove off. He never came back.

She went through it alone. Without him. Her family, her friends, her church—they were all there. But not her husband. Not the one she loved and needed most by her side. Where was he, this man she gave her heart to so long ago?

"Will you love her, comfort her, honor and keep her, in sickness and in health; and, forsaking all others, be faithful to her as long as you both shall live?"

"I will."[1]

But he didn't. He left her to suffer and die alone. Without him.

What if this is it? What if the most important questions in life revolve not around what we do to produce, but how we spend ourselves in relationships with others, for others, beginning with our relationship with the Lord, the One who matters most? What if faithfulness is more important than productiveness?

This is what the Lord said to Abraham: "Bring Me a three year old heifer, and a three year old female goat, and a three year old ram, and a turtledove, and a young pigeon" (Gen. 15:9).

Abraham knew exactly what was happening and what to do. "Then he brought all these to Him and cut them in two, and laid each half opposite the other; but he did not cut the birds" (Gen. 15:10).

This is it. This is the day that towers above all others throughout the entire recording of the Old Testament. Why? Because this is the day the Old Testament is enacted. It happens! The word *testament* is one and the same as the word *covenant* or *contract*. The Lord, the God of Abraham, is entering into a formal contract, a legal agreement, between Himself and Abraham.

Like we do in marriage.

Just like it was in the beginning. The Lord took the man and woman, who were two, and made them one (Gen. 2:24).

And now here it is. The Lord, by His own initiative, is entering into the same kind of formal, legal, covenant relationship with Abraham and his offspring. He is doing with us what He taught us to do with each other in marriage.

On this day, the Lord is entering into a covenant relationship with His people.

And how does the ceremony begin?

Back in that day, it began with bringing animals for sacrifice. Animals that would be cut in two and laid opposite of each other so that both parties, in making their vows, would pass "between these pieces" (Gen. 15:17; see Jer. 34:18).

Why the sacrifices? Simple truth: Relationships cost everything.

The death those animals died, the blood they shed, became a picture—a symbol—of the essence of what legal, covenant relationship is all about: We die to ourselves. We give ourselves fully and completely to the one we love. We surrender all that we are.

And that's exactly what we say today.

"I give you this ring as a symbol of my vow, and with all that I am, and all that I have, I honor you."[2]

What if this is it? What if this is what it's all about? What if the Lord has one thing in mind for us, one thing only? That we love Him first. Always. Forever. Daily. And that we passionately, faithfully, love each other?

Then, with His love in our heart, we go out and love a world in desperate need?

What if we've got it all wrong?

QUESTIONS FOR REFLECTION

Is your identity wrapped up in what you do? Are you known for how much you love or how much you produce?

Why can't we stay faithful in relationships? Why is it so hard to "die to ourselves"?

NOTES

1. Adapted from *The Book of Common Prayer* (Oxford: Oxford University Press, 1979), 424.

2. Ibid., 427.

26

PROMISES, REAL PROMISES

Reflections on Genesis 17:7–8

I will establish My covenant between Me and you and
your descendants after you throughout their generations
for an everlasting covenant, to be God to you
and to your descendants after you.

—GENESIS 17:7

Did he have his fingers crossed? Did she? Did their vows mean anything? They gave themselves to each other, forever. Their love declared, no matter what, through it all, until death do them part. Was it just the feeling in the moment? So when things change, feelings shift, the magic disappears, we're out? Is there fine print at the end of the contract?

Whatever happened to the old phrase: "One's word once given is binding"?

And so it happened, it really happened, the bride came down the aisle in all her beauty. The groom waiting to receive her. The church packed, standing, and joyful. The pastor ready to officiate the ceremony.

Did she just say, "Faithful, as long as we both shall *love*?" Maybe she's nervous. She misspoke unintentionally.

But then, did he just do the same thing? Did he just say, "Faithful, as long as we both shall *love*"?

The pastor was horrified. He had a choice right then and there, and he took it. He excused himself and the couple. He told the musicians to play and they went off through a door in the front of the church.

Two words. One vowel distinguishing them. "Which is it?" the pastor asked sharply. "As long as you both shall love? Or as long as you both shall live?" The couple was caught.

Yes, they had planned it. Yes, they wanted an escape clause in their vows so if they fell out of love they wouldn't be bound for life.

Five minutes later, they were back in front of the church. They repeated their vows. This time, they did it right. Fingers crossed.

Is it possible that this is it? That relationships rise or fall on a single vowel?

What if the world is constructed this way? What if the core design, the basic structure of the universe, rests on this relational principle "as long as we both shall love"? Imagine it, a world that only promises love today. Right now. Deeply. Passionately. But never binding. No commitment for tomorrow.

Maybe it goes something like this: We're in love today. A few years later, out of love. A few years later, back in love but with someone new. We're head over heels in love! Feels like forever love until the one we love actually falls out of love with us and finds a new love to love.

As long as we both shall love.

And the impact on our children?

Of course we love them. But if we think about it, the same goes for them too. It's not binding. It's love without commitment. They have to take it all in stride. When Mom leaves. Or Dad. Then comes a new mom. New dad. New school. Weekends with one. Weekdays with another. Big hugs with funny words: "We love you for as long as we love you."

A world where nothing is safe. Where trust is never known.

So imagine this is who God is. That when the Bible says, "God is love" (1 John 4:8, 16), it means this kind of fickle, feeling-based, no commitment, no promise for the future kind of love. Imagine that He entered into a legal, binding covenant with Abraham and all his descendants with this "never forever" kind of love.

What if He said to us, "As long as we both shall love"? So that's it? There when He feels like it. Gone when He doesn't?

Surprising, isn't it? This might actually reflect how many people perceive God. We go to Him when we need Him. When our lives are a stormy mess and we can't handle the junk of life. But the moment things turn around, things go well and the sun pops out, we're gone.

Fingers crossed.

But is He? That's the question: Is He like us? Are His promises like our promises? What does the Bible mean when it says "God is love"?

Here it is, the incomprehensible! A love story like no other the world has ever known. The Lord, the God of heaven and earth, takes to Himself the picture of the Bridegroom in pursuit of His bride.

And here is what the Bridegroom does: He enters into a covenant—a binding, legal, marital covenant with His people—and He makes promises, *real* promises. With real words like *faithfulness*, *compassion*, and *forever*. "I will betroth you to Me forever; yes, I will betroth you to Me in righteousness and in justice, in lovingkindness and in compassion, and I will betroth you to Me in faithfulness. Then you will know the LORD" (Hos. 2:19–20).

This is our God. He is faithful. He is trustworthy. He promises, "as long as we both shall live," and then He promises us forever. A real forever. Because when He speaks, His word is binding. His commitment is true because it is not based on a fickle, feeling-based passing whim in the moment. It's based on Him. His character. And He not only gives love, He is love. This kind of love.

Though we may come and go, love Him then leave Him, He remains faithful, always faithful. Trustworthy, always trustworthy. And that's how the story goes. At the end of time, there He stands, the Bridegroom, with His most beautiful bride. A people of His own choosing, bought with a great price.

No fingers crossed.

Imagine it. Imagine life with promises, real promises.

QUESTIONS FOR REFLECTION

Fingers crossed? Have you ever done that? Have you ever made promises that were not really promises at all?

This real God with real promises—do you trust Him? Do you believe His love is unconditional for you? If not, why not?

27

WE'RE TALKING 100 PERCENT

Reflections on Genesis 15:12–21

*It came about when the sun had set, that it was very dark,
and behold, there appeared a smoking oven and a
flaming torch which passed between these pieces.*

—GENESIS 15:17

First flight on a Friday morning from New York City to
Myrtle Beach.

The plane loaded with golfers. Middle-aged men with
1:00 p.m. tee times.

Drinks at 9:45 a.m.? Loud, frat-party jokes and laughing.
"Left the wife and kids at home!" a guy told me. "This is
my time. Four days of absolute freedom! No work. No wife
and kids telling me what to do. All year I look forward to
this weekend with my buddies. It's going to be a blast!"

Freedom!

"Does your wife mind?" I asked.

"You kiddin'?" he snorted back. "She hates it. She
barely spoke to me this morning. But I don't care. I work
hard all year. I bust my butt to make ends meet. I deserve
this. I earned this. One stinkin' weekend a year. That's all
I ask. Four days just me and my buddies. Golfin'. Drinkin'.

Partying like the good old days! What can be better than that?"

Freedom!

I pictured his wedding. Holding her hand, saying his vows, declaring his undying love. "And, oh, by the way. I get a weekend off once a year. Four days with my college buddies. Golfin' and drinkin'. Wanted you to know up front!"

She bats her eyes with understanding. "So we're talking 97 percent for the marriage thing, right? You get 3 percent off to go do whatever you do. Back to the single, college, party life. And I get the same. Is that it? Is that what we're saying?"

Does he nod and seal the deal? Or does he go for 4 percent off? Maybe 5 percent?

Wait a second. She gets time off too?

This poor man next to me on the plane lives for a weekend a year. He tells me he feels trapped at work. Trapped at home. Trapped with bills and a ton of responsibilities on his shoulders. Everyone pulling and tugging. Life stinks, plain and simple. But what doesn't stink? A weekend like this! A weekend to pretend he's twenty-two again. Fatter. Grayer. But just as free.

There's one piece of this story I get. The need for space. For time. It's part of what we do when we love someone. We help them find time for themselves. But it's way different than what this guy is talking about. This is something that's done together. It's supposed to be mutual—out of kindness and consideration for each other. It's part of the 100 percent, not less.

But this is what sin is all about. Self demanding self first, at the expense of others, of those we love. Even when we've pledged our all, our everything, there's the constant battle inside crying out, "What's in it for me?"

And we call that time off "freedom"?

How is it possible that God would ever enter into a relationship with people like us? And not just any relationship, we're talking a legal, covenant, contracted, marriage-like relationship. That's what the Old Testament or old covenant is all about. By His own doing, God entered into covenant with Abraham (Gen. 15:18).

Why do it? Look at the shape we're in. Selfish, demanding, me-first us. Not exactly faithful. Not exactly able to give 100 percent.

So what does the Lord do? As the ceremony begins, He puts Abraham to sleep (Gen. 15:12). He wants us to know how real covenant relationships work.

Traditionally, when covenants were made, the ceremony began like this: The animals for sacrifice would be slaughtered, cut in two (called the "sacred beriyth," the cutting of the covenant), signifying the death of our old selves. The two parties would then pass between the pieces. They would speak out loud their vows, make their pledges, giving themselves in full and complete surrender to the other as equals. They would then exchange certain possessions which symbolize that all they have, all they are, is now shared together (see 1 Sam. 18:1–5).

It's how covenants in the Bible were made. It's how the two become joined.

That said, just as Abraham is about to walk through the ceremony, the Lord steps in and puts him to sleep. A deep, terrifying sleep. Then, suddenly, two images appear: a smoking oven and a flaming torch, passing between the pieces. For Abraham. On behalf of Abraham. But not Abraham.

Who are they? Why is Abraham sleeping?

It's all going to make sense later, when the Messiah comes (see Luke 22:20).[1] But for now, one thing is clear. This covenant, and all its promises, rests fully and completely on God Himself. It does not rest on Abraham. Not in his own ability. Not whether he can do the 100 percent thing.

First things first. Abraham sleeps. The Lord is doing this—He is making a covenant.

Just like He did in the beginning. He took the man. He took the woman. He made them one by His own doing. And what He joins together—by His might and by His strength—is unbreakable (see Mark 10:6–9). His power does the joining. Covenant relationships never rest on our ability first.

They rest on His.

He's the One who makes relationships possible. It's Him. Always Him. We're talking 100 percent.

So when self demands self first, when our relationships begin to crumble way beyond our control, we know what to do. We know where to go. And it's not a once-a-year weekend away. It's not finding freedom outside the covenant. It's finding freedom inside.

We need Him. We need Him at the center of all our relationships. It's the only way to find real freedom.

It's the only way to give ourselves 100 percent.

QUESTIONS FOR REFLECTION

Is Jesus Christ at the center of your relationships? Is He what makes them possible?

Is He the one you, and those you're in relationship with, turn to for healing, grace, and reconciling power? Do you believe He can—He will—make things right?

NOTE

1. Luke 22:20 is where Jesus announced the new covenant; see also Galatians 3:15–18 for the apostle Paul's exposition of these verses. Dr. Allen Ross gives a brilliant commentary on the "fiery elements passing between the animals." By God Himself enacting this covenant, He "guarantees his people that his promises will be fulfilled." Allen P. Ross, *Creation and Blessing: A Guide to the Study and Exposition of Genesis*, rev. ed. (Grand Rapids, Mich.: Baker, 1996), 312–313.

28

THE BREAKABLE UNBREAKABLE

Reflections on Mark 10:1–9

*For this reason a man shall leave his father and mother,
and the two shall become one flesh; so they are no
longer two, but one flesh. What therefore God has
joined together, let no man separate.*

—MARK 10:7–9

Years ago, a man sat in my office, sobbing uncontrollably.

He had found the fence, the boundary line. Of course, that alone should have scared him away. But it didn't. He came right up to it. Felt it with his hands. Before he could really take time to think it through, the impulse seized him and he jumped it.

Straight into the arms of another woman.

He tried to replay the scene for me. Why he did what he did. Trying to find some reason, some excuse. It was a business trip. Couple of drinks. It just happened. Almost like he had no control of the moment. Even as he said it to me, he knew it wasn't true. He knew what he was doing. He just thought no one would ever know. That his wife wouldn't find out.

All he saw was pleasure in the moment. Confidence that he could handle it afterwards. A quiet whisper over his shoulder telling him he can easily jump back over the fence in the morning, and that will be that. As if it never happened.

Complete control. Arrogant self-confidence. The good, church-going husband and father doing in the dark what will *never* come out in the light.

Morning came. The business meetings that day went on as scheduled. Then the flight home, the first sight of his three little boys as he walked in the house, the first embrace of his wife. All normal. As if it never happened. And it almost worked. He almost got away with it.

But the guilt inside his soul was too strong for him. He needed me to help him, to tell him to do something, anything, to make it go away. In the crazy, mixed-up world of his mind, he wasn't trying to get right with God. Sadly, tragically, that didn't concern him. He needed to get back over the fence to his wife, which now seemed impossible. He still felt like he was on the wrong side. And the fence kept growing bigger and bigger. It was way too high to cross over.

"Do you think," he asked, "God will help me? Will He fix my marriage? I can't lose her. I can't lose my boys."

I did my best to give counsel. I redirected the conversation to the only One who can speak into moments like these. But it was to no avail. He didn't want to hear it. Only one thing mattered to him. He had to get rid of the guilt. He had to tell his wife and come clean. And that's what he did. A year later, the divorce was finalized.

Fences.[1] There are fixed boundaries in covenant relationships.

On the one hand, unbreakable. In the marital bond, the words go like this: "What therefore God has joined together, let no man separate" (Mark 10:9). This is it. It's His work. He takes the two and makes them one.

On the other hand, there is this *if* word: "If you do this, then . . ." There are ways to break the unbreakable. There are fences, boundaries. So if we do the unthinkable, if we leap the fence and commit the immoral act of giving our body, our heart, our soul to another, we break the covenant. And the soul, the conscience—if it hasn't frozen hard and cold—knows it.

This is exactly how the Bible speaks of the unbreakable covenant with Him. It is just that—unbreakable. The promises God made to Abraham were passed down to Isaac and Jacob and the children of Israel. All of His promises, the apostle Paul said, find their yes and amen in Jesus Christ (2 Cor. 1:20).

He has called a people to Himself. He has rescued us, saved us, and if we truly belong to Him, He has put His resurrected life into our mortal bodies causing us to be in Christ and Christ in us by the Holy Spirit, born from above (Rom. 8:11; 2 Cor. 5:17; Gal. 2:20; 1 Pet. 1:3).

We are His. He is ours. Forever. And that by His doing. But that doesn't mean we get to do what we want when we want.

Deep inside the old covenant stands the *if*. If we obey the Lord our God. If we turn to Him with all our heart and soul, *then* we live. But if our heart turns away, if we are drawn away to worship other gods, then we die.

"See I have set before you today life . . . and death. . . . So choose life" (Deut. 30:15, 19).

Just as deep inside the new covenant stands the powerful *if*. We who belong to Christ Jesus are not allowed to "continue in sin" (Rom. 6:1). It is wrong, ungodly thinking to think that if we're Christians we're done with fences. To think to ourselves, "We can do what we want when we want because Jesus has saved us." If we think this way, then we need time in Hebrews 10:26–27: "For if we go on sinning willfully after receiving the knowledge of the truth, there no longer remains a sacrifice for sins, but a terrifying expectation of judgment and the fury of a fire which will consume the adversaries."

Fences. There are fences, boundary lines. Stay inside and we find what the Bible calls blessings. Leap outside and the Bible calls it curses.

But thanks be to God who has poured out the Holy Spirit into our hearts to guard us from leaping fences. He has given us the body of Christ, our brothers and sisters, to come around us in times of temptation. He has given us His Word to light our way. He has provided perfect access to His throne. (See Rom. 5:5; Gal. 6:1–2; 2 Tim. 3:15–17; Heb. 4:16.)

He knows how to keep His own. He knows how to keep the unbreakable unbreakable in our relationship to Him, in our marriages, and in our relationships to others. That's what He does.

And He is *always* faithful.

But don't think there aren't fences. Don't get cocky and overconfident and wake up one morning on the wrong side of the fence. And if this happens, don't turn your heart away from Him. He's the only One, in times like that, who knows what to do.

Instead, run to Him—lest you get caught in that terrifying world where the unbreakable breaks.

QUESTIONS FOR REFLECTION

Hidden in this story is the seductive power of the Tempter who lures us to cross fences and promises that we can keep it secret. Do you know something about fence crossing?

Too often our preaching makes light of betrayal. But breaking covenant breaks the heart. We need Jesus to help us in these things. Do you need Him today to help, to give grace, to heal your heart?

NOTE

1. I highly recommend the book by Denver Moore and Ron Hall, *Same Kind of Different as Me: A Modern-Day Slave, an International Art Dealer, and the Unlikely Woman Who Bound Them Together* (Nashville: Thomas Nelson, 2006). The heroine of the story is an extraordinary woman named Deborah Hall who, after the infidelity of her husband, set him on a path to Jesus Christ.

29

SEALED FROM ABOVE

Reflections on Genesis 17:9–14

*This is My covenant, which you shall keep, between Me
and you and your descendants after you: every male
among you shall be circumcised.*

—GENESIS 17:10

As 2010 came to a close, one person more than any
other stood out larger than life in our church family.

Sweet Miss Lydia.

Lydia died in April 2010 at the age of eight months.

She came into this world with a genetic disease called
Zellweger syndrome. It was so bad that her parents, Micah
and Jen, brought her home from the hospital at six weeks,
thinking she wouldn't make it through the weekend.

But she did. For a window in time, this little girl had
personality. She could burst through the confines of the
disease and the meds and show herself off! That unique,
God-crafted, one in a million, amazing-to-be-me kind of girl.

Until the window closed. The disease roared. The meds
tried and failed. And Miss Lydia was gone.

Her memorial service was packed. A ton of people went
on the journey with Micah, Jen, and Lydia. All the hospital

visits. Updates on their blog. Prayer warriors lifting this family to Jesus, walking into the valley of the shadow of death with them, trusting the Lord to give grace each day.

And then grace to go home to be with Jesus.

It's hard to go the journey. I guess some didn't get it. They came, they saw, they shook their head and said, "It's just so sad. I mean, really sad." Then closed their eyes, went on with life, pretending she never came.

Others I'm sure got mad at God. Another reason to walk away.

And others ran to Him. Not getting the why. Sometimes wishing we could close our eyes and wish it all away so we wouldn't hurt so much. Sometimes getting mad. But a different kind of mad. Not the kind that turns away from Him but the kind that runs full steam toward Him. That's the crazy part of grieving deep in Christ. Wanting to blame Him. Needing to be near Him. Both at the same time.

It's hard to go the journey.

Many marriages don't survive the death of a child. The wound in the soul cuts with such force that there's nothing left inside us. Nothing to give the one we love. So we push away.

It's like standing together on a bridge watching a tsunami come. It's just too big, too much power. The heart can't handle it. The bridge can't negotiate it.

Most couples don't survive this.

And the words that meant everything mean nothing. "What therefore God has joined together, let no man separate" (Mark 10:9).

Unless it happened. Unless these words weren't just words spoken at the time of marriage, but words accompanied by power. Real, tangible, physical power come down from heaven to make the two inseparably one. This gift of God, this joining together in a bond deeper than any wound can cut. Stronger than any tsunami can tear apart. Able to survive the unthinkable.

The loss of their own child.

I remember hearing a preacher once call it "cosmic glue." Can't see it. Can't really feel it. Can't know it's supernatural cosmic power until we're thrust into the dark valley. Battling through the disease. Standing at the graveside. Trying to live some semblance of life in the long days, weeks, and months that follow. That's when it's really known—in the testing.

It's either there or it isn't.

Sealed from above.

The Bible puts it in pictures. The seal of the old covenant was circumcision. A mark in the flesh. An outward sign of what the Lord does in the souls of all His people who believe. He calls it, "the circumcision of the heart" (see Deut. 10:16; 20:6; Jer. 4:4; 9:23–26; Rom. 2:28–29). The apostle Paul called the sign of circumcision to Abraham the "seal of the righteousness of the faith which he had while uncircumcised" (Rom. 4:11). He was sealed on the inside before the sign marked him on the outside. The righteousness that comes by faith was in him. Sealed forever.

"I will be their God, and they shall be My people" (Jer. 31:33).

The same is true in the new covenant. When we believe, when we're baptized and brought into Jesus Christ and His family, the circumcision is "of the heart, by the Spirit" (Rom. 2:29). We are sealed from above.

By the marks in His flesh.

Outward signs of an inward power that is like cosmic glue. The seal inside that guarantees no matter how fierce the storm, how deep the valley, we are safe in Christ. He with us. We with Him. Forever. Always.

So, in marriage, we give each other rings. Outward signs of our love for each other. But more. So much more. They are outward signs of the power of God come down from heaven, joining us. The Holy Spirit sealing us.

No matter how hard the journey is.

We need Him today. In our marriages. In our Christian relationships. In our relationship with the Lord. It's the only thing that gives us strength to live each day for Him. Even when the testing comes. And comes hard.

Jen and Micah know this. In a loss deeper than words will ever speak, it's there and they know it. Between them. And between them and Jesus. Forever. Always.[1]

The cosmic glue. Sealed from above.

QUESTIONS FOR REFLECTION

Is there cosmic glue between you and the Lord? Do you know your heart to be circumcised by an act of the Holy Spirit?

This glue belongs in our relationships—our covenant relationships, our families, our church families, our bond in Christ with others. Can you feel it? Do you need it?

NOTE

1. To know more about Zellweger syndrome, read the powerful testimony of Nancy and David Guthrie. Nancy Guthrie, *Holding On to Hope: A Pathway through Suffering to the Heart of God* (Wheaton, Ill.: Tyndale, 2002).

30

THE CHRISTMAS NAME

Reflections on Genesis 17:1–5

*No longer shall your name be called Abram, but your
name shall be Abraham; for I have made you the
father of a multitude of nations.*

—GENESIS 17:5

Anderson. She scribbled it while talking on the phone.
Then crossed it out.

It was actually her maiden name. But it didn't matter.
Everyone knew she was an Anderson. Now that the kids
were nearly grown, her husband off on his jet-set career, she
was trying to find her place in the world again. And in one
sense, it was all there. On a silver platter. If she wanted it.

But she didn't. It's true, people called for her to do this
project, do that cause, sign up with their company and be
the face. The image that could sell product. Maybe well-
intentioned, but she knew the reason they were calling. She
was an Anderson.

That's what they saw. Not her, but the name. Somewhere
along the way, she lost something of herself, and she couldn't
seem to find it again. So she kept smiling at all the flattery,
then gently, kindly, said no and walked away.

Too many years of being what everyone wanted her to be.

So she broke free. She did what people didn't expect. Hurt some. Surprised others. Not because she had all the answers, but because she didn't, and she needed to find them. And she might have, if there had been more time.

But there wasn't. She had cancer. The inoperable, incurable kind. She really didn't have much of a choice. She folded back into her family again where she was deeply loved and cared for until she died a few months later.

Anderson.

Some names we choose. Some we don't. In some cultures, at the time of marriage, the woman takes the name of her husband. In other cultures, it's all found in a hyphen. He takes her name. She takes his. The "who they are" is all bound up in each other. It's the whole point of the two becoming one. To leave father and mother. To cleave to each other.

New name. New identity. Old things passed away. New things come.

Name change is part of that story. Name change is huge.

Too often it's what we do because it's what we're expected to do and we miss the enormity of it all. Our names are who we are. Where we've come from. The people we belong to. The things our families have done. Who we've made ourselves to be. It's how we're known. It's how we've always been known.

Put down. Laid aside. All of it.

And there's more. We take the name of the one we love. We lose ourselves so completely only to find ourselves in the identity of another. Their story. Their history. Their people. Their future. Love a thousand times beyond a feeling. Love that is real sacrifice. The gift of ourselves, all of ourselves, to another.

I think of the words of Ruth, a great woman of the Bible, who declared her love to Naomi, her mother-in-law: "Do not urge me to leave you or turn back from following you; for where you go, I will go, and where you lodge, I will lodge. Your people shall be my people, and your God, my God. Where you die, I will die, and there I will be buried. Thus may the LORD do to me, and worse, if anything but death parts you and me" (Ruth 1:16–17).

This is love like no other.

And it's what *both* are supposed to do. Not just one. This declaration of selfless, sacrificial love is mutual. In a perfect world, both lose their names. Both take on new names. Old identities gone. New identities come. Never one without the other. It's both, always both. A two-way street.

Anderson.

It wasn't two-way anymore. Not for her. Her maiden name and her married name had somehow morphed into a glittering outward show. A face, an image, a demanding expectation she'd smile for society. And then applaud her husband's new mistress—his career. Not her. She was so lost inside. So empty.

She had come to hate her name.

It's supposed to be a two-way street, right?

It was two-way when the Lord entered into covenant with Abraham. He changed his name. The old name, Abram

(Gen. 17:5).[1] His new name, Abraham.[2] He did the same with Sarah, changing her name from Sarai (Gen. 17:15).[3] And then He did it Himself. He took on their name. From that point on and forever, He'd be called the God of Abraham. His name forever bound to Abraham's.

And then He did more. His plan was bigger, beyond anything we could ever imagine and dream. How is it even possible to understand this?

On Christmas morning, He was registered in the census. His family name went back to King David. Then to Abraham, Noah, Enoch, and Adam. He belonged to our race, our people, our bloodline. He was every bit Immanuel—the fullness of the Godhead wrapped in the tiniest blankets.

Jesus. Of the town of Nazareth. Born of a woman. Just like us.

He took on our name so that we might take on His. He bound Himself to us in what He called "the new covenant in [His] blood" that all those without a name, the lost and broken of heart, the empty and bankrupt of soul, might have a name, a new name (Luke 22:20; 1 Cor. 11:25). A new identity that lasts forever. That we might give ourselves to Him as He gave Himself to us.

Love like no other.

Found in Jesus, the name far above all other names.

The Christmas name.

QUESTIONS FOR REFLECTION

In past generations, the newly baptized would be given a Christian name. It would signify their identity is now found in Jesus Christ and His people. Is that your identity too?

Does it move you? Does it stir love in your heart, to know that He—in this covenant with you—takes on your name as His name?

NOTES

1. Abram means "exalted father." Old Testament scholar, Allen Ross, suggests this name signifies Abram's descent from an exalted father: "That is, he was of distinguished lineage and high birth." Allen P. Ross, *Creation and Blessing: A Guide to the Study and Exposition of Genesis* (Grand Rapids, Mich.: Baker, 1996), 331.

2. Abraham means "the father of a multitude" and signifies that God not only placed His promises into Abraham's name, but also His own name which guarantees their fulfillment.

3. Sarah's new name means "princess" or "queen" from whom kings would come, and not just kings, but the King of Kings Himself.

31

AT ARM'S LENGTH

~~~

Reflections on Jeremiah 31:31–34

*"Behold, days are coming," declares the LORD, "when
I will make a new covenant with the house of Israel
and with the house of Judah."*

—JEREMIAH 31:31

A couple had come to visit my wife and me. A dear
friend of theirs had moved away and they were grieving.
They allowed me to share their story:

We had been so close for so long.

When he made the choice to leave, we did
everything we could to come around him. Our
fellowship is full of strong Christians who are
compassionate, concerned, and ready to stand with
him no matter what. We had hoped to talk this matter
out together—if he'd let us.

He'd received a new job offer promising a new
world had opened up for him. A big world, promising
huge success, money, affluence, and a name bigger
than life. For whatever reason, he chose to keep quiet
about it and not invite us to talk with him or pray

with him, like we've always done together. He simply made his decision and then told us, asking for only one thing—that we'd be happy for him.

It's hard to explain why it hurt so much. We'd been together such a long time. Our sharing had become deep. We learned not only to pray together, but to hear the Lord together. A profound trust had been built, which allowed us the freedom to hold each other accountable and speak truthfully into each other's lives.

And that trust grew as we served together in ministry. We had done mission trips all over the world. We saw the Lord work powerfully in a thousand different ways. The more we did, the closer we became. There's nothing quite like it—to walk together in Christ.

So this was a real shock for us. Not just that he took the job and left, but that we weren't allowed to be with him in the process. Really, to be the body of Christ for him.

Instead, he kept us at arm's length.

We asked him about it. But he told us that his decision was made and that we needed to accept it, be happy for him, and pray for him as he goes. And we did.

But we miss him deeply. And, to be honest, we're concerned for him. Why did he push us away after all these years? It felt like something wasn't right. For reasons we're still working through, we felt the bond of trust break. We just felt hurt.

We still do.

Kept at arm's length.

I know why I stick out my arm. Not just with those close to me, but with the Lord Himself. It's usually because I don't want to hear what they have to say.

Like I've made up my mind. Because "I'm going to do what I'm going to do."

A friend of mine said it this way: "Sometimes I don't want to get too close to the Lord because I'm afraid of what He's going to say. He's going to deal with things I don't want Him to deal with."

But that's what He does. And that's the gospel story. The incredible story. He chooses to come close. Intimately close. It's why He entered into a covenant relationship with Abraham saying, "I am God Almighty; walk before Me, and be blameless" (Gen. 17:1).

Now that's close!

Just like the days of Eden when the Lord walked "in the garden in the cool of the day" (Gen. 3:8). This dynamic communion. The intimate fellowship with Adam and Eve. They walked together in the light of the Lord. All things open. Nothing hidden in secret. For this we were created.

But you know the story. I know the story. Sin broke that fellowship.

This is why the word *covenant* is such a huge word in the Bible. The old covenant established with Abraham and his offspring. The new covenant established by our Lord Jesus Christ at Passover meal. This is the testimony: The Lord has chosen to enter into relationship with us.

Close. Real close.

Once, sin—our sin—put us at arm's length from God and from each other. But now, no more because the Lord did what we ourselves could not do: "And I will be their God, and they shall be My people" (Jer. 31:33).

He demonstrated this when He placed His sanctuary square in the middle of the people of Israel. He did this for one purpose: "that [He] may dwell among them" (Ex. 25:8).

Again, close. Real close. It is His plan. Always His plan. For all eternity.

"Behold, the tabernacle of God is among men, and He will dwell among them, and they shall be His people, and God Himself will be among them" (Rev. 21:3).

His plan for you, His plan for me: We are never, never to put Him at arm's length. Never, never to put each other at arm's length.

So, why do we do it?

Out comes the arm—pushing away those we love, those we trust because we don't want to hear. Because, deep down, we want to do what we want to do and we're going to do it without anyone stopping us.

Or maybe it happens to us. We get the stiff arm. We feel its impact and something in our heart breaks. Those we love push us away. Walk away. Stay away. And we're left to feel what God never intended us to feel.

Kept at arm's length.

QUESTIONS FOR REFLECTION

Can you feel it when someone keep you at arm's length? Are you aware when you do it to others, especially those close to you? Always?

The Lord has designed us to be in community, not alone and separate. Are you willing to let people in—to walk with you, pray with you, talk with you? Are there parts of your life you keep hidden, even from God?

32

AND THEN WE ATE AND DRANK

Reflections on Luke 22:14–23

And when He had taken some bread and given thanks,
He broke it and gave it to them, saying, "This is My body
which is given for you; do this in remembrance of Me."

—LUKE 22:19

I wish I knew why we hurt each other.

Years ago, a rumor started about my wife and me. It weaseled its way over to the coffee hour after church. It got picked up and passed along the phone lines the next week. A month went by before it was actually spoken out loud in the leaders' meeting. By then it was no longer a rumor but "fact."

Gossip dressed to kill.

It was "fact" not because it was a fact, but because no one took the time to find out if it was true. So it just morphed and re-morphed. Until it became bigger than life.

It's one thing to be on the sidelines watching it happen (which we're actually not supposed to do in the Lord). It's quite another to be the subject of the rumor. By the time we found out, it was too late for us to do anything about it.

Opinions had formed. Sides taken. Perceptions had turned magically into truth. People of reputation had spoken quietly on the matter. The senior pastor took note, though he decided not to say anything about it or take any action. It was as if a secret vote had been formally recommended, seconded, discussed, and then passed. Completely off the record.

The gossip was no longer gossip. And it hurt.

From a feeling perspective, it was like we were tossed out of the church. Branded as sinners. Oh we got smiles from everybody. Absolutely! It was like it never happened. But, in truth, we were pushed out of the family. We never received a fair hearing. We never had somebody come alongside and listen.

We tried to speak. Once. But like I said, it was too late. Too much gossip had piled on top of the original gossip making it all entirely too complicated. So when we did speak, because we forced the issue, demanding to be heard, we appeared defensive. Like we were speaking from hurt. Which was true. We were.

We felt trapped. There was nothing we could do. We went to church on Sunday mornings. We kept a low profile. We did our best to be faithful.

Months passed. A year passed. We decided it was best to quietly leave and attend another church. But, as God would have it, two years after the rumor took flight, dear friends of ours invited us to go to a conference where our former pastor was the keynote speaker. We actually wanted to go. We loved him so much. But should we? With all the hurt we had suffered?

Yes? No? Why go? It'll only bring it all back. The gossip. The disappointment. But we should go; we wanted to go.

We couldn't decide. Back and forth until, the morning the conference began, and we just did it.

We devised a secret little plan. We'd get there five minutes late. Sit in the back. Leave before he saw us. He would never know we were even there. Brilliant! Ingenious!

Great plan, but it didn't work. The room was packed. Ushers were seating latecomers. We were escorted up to the second row some ten feet away from the speaker's lectern. Of course.

We were horrified. This was completely not our plan. We wanted to grab our stuff and leave. But how could we? People around us were greeting us like they knew us. Way too friendly. We just looked at each other and sighed.

Awkward. Really, really awkward.

As our pastor came to pulpit and began teaching from the Scriptures, he saw us. He kept looking over at us with a genuine warmth and kindness. Almost as if he was glad to see us.

When he was done teaching, as the church went into prayer, I saw the bread and cup come out. They were going to offer Communion. We knew nothing about how this would work. But soon enough, it wasn't hard to figure out. Those dangerous ushers were back. They came to our row, nodded, and suddenly we were up, filing out of the pews, and heading forward to receive.

When it came time, we were told where to go. Of course, as if perfectly planned and divinely orchestrated, we were sent to our former pastor.

I thought to myself, "Just smile. Receive. And go."

But he opened his arms, smiled, and we didn't hesitate. We walked right into his gentle but strong embrace.

"My dear friends, I am sorry for what happened. But today, right now, right here, it's over. Completely over. All is forgiven. Like it never happened. The details don't matter. We surrender all of it to our Father in heaven. We lay it down at the cross of Jesus. Any hurt, any resentment for the gossip that tore us apart—all of it—is under the blood of Calvary and settled in the courts of heaven forever. Believe it and receive it."

After the service was over, he told us he'd go back to the church and tell the elders that the matter with the Barnums was over. He never wanted to hear the gossip about us mentioned ever again.

"It's over," he repeated. "It's really over."

I know the human condition in sin is strong inside us. For a fleeting second, there was a desire in me to want to argue out the fine points of the conflict. That carefully written speech had sadly gone around and around in my mind for months. But it was just a fleeting second. Something else was at work here. Something that belonged to God.

The Lord had stepped in. He stood with the three of us and we all knew it. By His grace, in His compassion and mercy, He reconciled us to each other in Jesus' name.

It was over. All of it. Our pastor said it so well when we were received back into the fellowship of the church a few Sundays later: "Washed in the blood. Cleansed by our Savior. Forgiven and more than forgiven—reconciled in Jesus Christ. The sin gone. Forever gone. We are family again."

And we were. Neither of us could explain the wonder of this moment. We both knew and felt the grace that came when the Lord reconciled us back together in Jesus. We—as a church family—had messed things up. But together, in Him, we found the power that comes from the Holy Spirit when we reconcile in His name and at the cross of Jesus.

And with that, our church family went to the table. We came together as the pastor took the bread and the cup and said the words of our Lord Jesus Christ, "Take, eat; this is My body. This is My blood of the covenant."

The covenant meal. This is the table of celebration given to us by God in Christ declaring that He Himself has come. He has borne the price of our rebellion and sin. He has entered into an everlasting covenant with us through Abraham and then, in its great fulfillment, through His Son, Jesus Christ.

The table was set. We were invited to eat with each other and with Him. And it was true. All is forgiven. It is settled in the courts of heaven forever.

And then—thanks be to God!—we ate and drank.

QUESTIONS FOR REFLECTION

In the ancient church, Christians were not allowed to come to Communion unless they were right with each other; they shared the peace of Christ first. Do you, today, have peace in your relationships?

When you don't, have you done everything you can on your part to reconcile? If the other party isn't willing, have you forgiven him or her? Are you praying for that person—and for reconciliation still to come?

PART 5

OBEDIENCE
IN JESUS

33

STANDING BEFORE THE LORD

Reflections on Genesis 18:16–33

*Abraham was still standing before the LORD. Abraham
came near and said, "Will You indeed sweep
away the righteous with the wicked?"*

—GENESIS 18:22–24

She had a place, a secret place, where she could close
the door, come before her Father in heaven, and weep.

One prayer, the same prayer, for months. For years. For
more than twenty-five years. She never gave up. She never
lost hope.

Her husband.

Early on in their marriage she had come to faith in Jesus
Christ. She had shared it all with her husband. The more
she grew in faith, delighted in Scripture, and saw the Lord
miraculously answer prayer, the more she told him. She
just kept on telling him.

A thousand times, she'd invite him to come to the
prayer meetings. A thousand times he pushed her away.

Until she realized the door was closed. Bolted shut. He
didn't want to hear it. Didn't want to talk about it. And
didn't like what was happening to her.

And so she stopped. They lived their lives, raised their kids, and shared everything together, except this. Not this. Never this. He had no problem with her attending the prayer meetings. As a matter of fact, he wanted her to go. It made him look good. On Sunday mornings, he even encouraged people to go.

You see, he was the minister, the senior pastor of the church. He was the Sunday morning preacher. The seminary graduate. The writer, theologian, and brilliant scholar. Regarded by his colleagues as a leader among leaders.

No one knew what his wife knew.

No one knew the grief she bore. She couldn't tell anyone. How could she? So she ran to her place, her secret place, day after day, year after year, coming before the Lord, weeping for her husband, praying the same prayer: "Lord Jesus, save my husband."

Every once in a while it came out of her mouth. In weak moments. Angry moments. Moments she'd wish she could take back. But she'd say it to his face: "I'm praying for you. Praying that Jesus will save you."

Nothing infuriated him more. Nothing pushed him further away. He'd come back just as fast: "Who are you to say that to me?"

The rift only deepened over time. In a moment of self-vindication, he boasted in being elected to the office of bishop in the Anglican Church. He told her how many leaders and honored dignitaries in the church believed him to be a good and godly man. "Everyone," he'd tell her, "except you!"

She never stopped praying. Her tears bitter. Her heart broken before the Lord.

Prayer—it is the privilege of those who are bound to His covenant.

This is exactly what Abraham did for his nephew Lot. In the early days of the Bible, as the Lord was teaching His people about what it means to be in a covenant relationship with Him, He allowed access into His presence.

Later, in the days of Moses, He would be more specific. But for now, He wanted Abraham to know that he could come and stand before Him. And so, in Genesis 18, the Lord appeared to Abraham. He said, as if thinking to Himself, "Shall I hide from Abraham what I am about to do?" (Gen. 18:17).

The Lord shared His heart concerning Sodom and Gomorrah. The time of judgment had come upon them for the enormity of their sin and wickedness.

But what about Lot? That's where Lot and his family lived.

The Bible says that Abraham stood before the Lord and began to speak to Him: "Will You indeed sweep away the righteous and the wicked? Suppose there are fifty righteous within the city. . . . Suppose forty are there? . . . Thirty . . . twenty . . . ten?" (Gen. 18:23–32).

Abraham was learning the most honored privilege of a covenant child of God. We are given permission to stand before Him. To speak to Him. To pray and intercede for others.

Just like this woman did for her husband, the pastor.

Well after the children were gone, with families of their own, and well after her husband had established himself as one of the most respected ministers and church leaders of his time, he slipped into a quiet sin. He thought he had control of it, but he didn't. No one knew the addiction that enslaved him. He was that good. He brilliantly hid it from those closest to him. But he knew and he knew God knew. And he knew, soon enough, the world would know too. He had to do something. But what?

As he watched his wife pack her bags to attend a three-day prayer conference, he surprised her and said, "I'm going with you."

"You won't like it," she said as a matter of fact.

But he went anyway. He packed his bags. He drove with her to the airport. He walked into the conference and entered a world where no one knew he was a minister. Just a man. A husband trying, after all these years, to support his wife.

She was never clear when it happened. Or how. But at some point in the conference, the Lord answered her twenty-five-year-old prayer. He opened her husband's heart. At first, the man felt fear. Fear that his ministry had been a sham. Fear that everything he'd done, everything he'd built, everything he'd believed, was about to crumble into a pile of rubble around him. He didn't want that. He could feel himself resisting, turning away.

But the Lord's hand was strong on him. So strong that tears began filling his eyes. All these years, he knew his wife had been praying for him, weeping for him, that he'd come to know Jesus and be saved by Him. Real. Deep. Alive. And he had laughed at her, pushing her away.

He was stuck. If he stayed, he'd have to face his fears. If he left, he'd have to deal with an addiction that was strangling him at his very core. He didn't know what to do. Except get on his knees. And let Him come. Let Him help him.

And He did.

"I don't know how it's possible," he testified at the very end of the conference, "to be a seminary graduate, a pastor of churches, a theologian and bishop in the church of Jesus Christ and not know Him as I know Him now. My Lord. My Savior. My God. But I am here to say—it grieves me to say—it is possible. My wife has spent decades in prayer for me. And here, standing before you, I tell you—her prayers have been answered. I came here suffering from an addiction I couldn't handle alone. I leave here . . . not alone."

With that, he sat down and wept.

QUESTIONS FOR REFLECTION

It doesn't seem imaginable that the Lord knows us so intimately—and hears and meets us as we come to Him in prayer. Have you considered this great privilege that is yours in Christ?

If our identity is found in God—that is, who we are rests on who He is and what He's done for us—then prayer is everything. Are you going to Him, both privately and with brothers and sisters in Christ? Is prayer everything to you?

34

GOD TESTED ABRAHAM

~~~

Reflections on Genesis 22:1

Now it came about after these things, that God tested Abraham, and said to him, "Abraham!" And he said, "Here I am."

—GENESIS 22:1

It's a fact of life. We're tested.

We expect it at work. Many of us have quarterly or yearly evaluations to see if our work meets the required standards of excellence. We find out if we're at our best. If we've kept focus. If we're giving 100 percent.

We expect it in life. Sometimes we bring the testing on ourselves. We make bad decisions. We do the wrong thing. We hurt others and ourselves, and we pay for it. Real actions that lead to real consequences.

Other times the testing comes from the outside.

I will never forget the day we had to go to the hospital to see Allie.

She was in her early eighties. The infection in her lungs was nearly gone. But the doctors thought it best to keep her in the hospital one more night for observation. One more night.

By the time my wife and I got there she was already dressed, sitting in the chair, ready for discharge. I couldn't help but think to myself, "How does anyone do this? It's just doesn't feel right. Or fair. Let the young be tested. The middle aged. The early seniors while they're still fully surrounded by friends and family. But not this. Not in her old age."

She was so happy to see us. She was talking a mile a minute, telling us everything the doctors had said; how much she wanted to go home; the plans she had for the week and the people she couldn't wait to call. Jenny, her daughter, she told us, was coming to get her any minute. She was hoping they might stop and get something to eat at a favorite restaurant before going home.

"Allie, we've got news. Bad news."

We told her that in the early morning hours her house caught fire. There was nothing the firefighters could do. Everything was destroyed.

"Jenny?" she asked.

She had come home to live with her mother after her husband had left her and the divorce was final. Her bedroom was on the first floor but somehow, rather than going out the window to safety, she opened the door of her bedroom and was engulfed in the flames.

"She's gone, Allie. She died in the fire."

Everything was gone. A lifetime of possessions, photos, memories shared with her husband who had passed away some years back. This was their house and now it was all gone. But nothing compared to the overwhelming loss of her Jenny.

"Jenny's dead?" she kept asking. "I should have been there. I was supposed to be released yesterday. The doctors told me to stay one more night. I should have been there. Are you sure? Jenny's dead?"

It's a fact of life. We're tested.

It's almost as if it doesn't matter where the testing comes from. Inevitably, we are face-to-face with the hardest questions of life — and whether we'll go into them with the Lord. Will we trust Him in all that we have to go through? Is He everything to us?

Maybe it's easier and even right to say that Allie's testing came because we live in a broken, fallen world where accidents, fires, wars, tornadoes, and earthquakes happen. It allows us to blame the tragedy on circumstance.

Or we can say the Devil did this. Just like he did with Job.

It's hard to say the words: God tested Allie.

But this is exactly what happened to Abraham. The Bible says: "God tested Abraham." The Lord called out to him, "Abraham!" And he said back, "Here I am" (Gen. 22:1).

A time of testing. In his old age.

It wasn't the first time. In the beginning, when the Lord first appeared to him, He called Abraham to leave his homeland and follow Him. And Abraham said yes. He obeyed and "went out, not knowing where he was going" (Heb. 11:8).

Over and over again, the Lord called Abraham to follow Him, to trust Him, to obey Him. And each step of the way, sometimes faltering here, faltering there, Abraham did what was right.

Now, in his old age, he was finally enjoying his son Isaac. The miracle son. The son the Lord had promised. The son through whom Abraham would become the father of nations.

Why test him now? Why not let Abraham live out his days in peace? And why doesn't Abraham say what I want him to say at a time like this, "Tell me why, Lord. Tell me why."

But Abraham didn't ask why. He said simply, "Here I am."

And that's exactly what Allie did. She left the hospital that day knowing the Lord would be with her in her pain. He had been faithful to her for as long as she could remember and she knew now, in the worst tragedy of her life, that He would be faithful to her again.

"But did she suffer?" Allie asked the bishop of Pittsburgh at Jenny's funeral. "I'm having bad dreams of her walking into the fire."

The bishop took Allie's hands and, with such kindness in his voice, he assured her of the one thing we all knew so well—Jenny loved Jesus. She had known Him and served Him since she was a child. She didn't just walk into the fire. She walked into the arms of her Savior.

Allie would later say that those words brought healing to her soul. Never again would she have dreams of her daughter suffering.

She lived another five or so years. She missed Jenny terribly. She grieved her loss to the day she died. But even then, she kept doing the one thing she knew to do. She put her trust in the Lord. She knew Him to be faithful, always faithful. And, she'd tell us, He never failed her. Not once.

Here I am, said Allie. Here I am.

QUESTIONS FOR REFLECTION

The words seem impossible to say: God is testing me. But there are times it's true. And the question that we each face is this: Can I say with Abraham, "Here I am, Lord"?

How can you be ready to say, no matter the tragedy, "You are faithful, Lord, always faithful. And I trust You as I've always trusted You"? Do you want this in your life? Will you ask Him for it? If not, why not?

35

STANDING BETWEEN

Reflections on Genesis 22:2

*He said, "Take now your son, your only son, whom you love,
Isaac, and go to the land of Moriah, and offer him there as a
burnt offering on one of the mountains of which I will tell you."*

—Genesis 22:2

Testing has always one piercing focus: Where is our heart?

When God tested Abraham, He demanded his son, his only son, the son he deeply loved. Is it possible that Abraham's heart had shifted? That somehow his son Isaac had become everything to him? More than life itself? More than God Himself?

Is it possible that our heart shifts?

It did for Kathryn. She grew up in a time when itinerant evangelists would travel from town to town, set up their tents, gather the crowds, and stay for weeks. Nothing captured her heart more. She loved Jesus. She loved to speak His name. With a burning in her heart, she wanted the world to know Him.

Maybe it was odd for a young woman in the mid-1930s to leave her home and travel through the Midwest with tent revivalists. But she didn't seem to care about that. She knew the call of Jesus Christ on her life. She witnessed night after night the testimonies of people coming to faith in Him. She dreamed big. Bigger tents. Bigger towns. To win cities for Christ.

Until, that is, the love of her life stepped into the picture. The man she adored. And what could be better than this? He too loved Jesus. He too had a call of God on his life to do nothing else but travel the country, gather crowds, and tell people what Jesus Christ had done for them.

They married in October 1938.

Here's the glitch. He was married with two children. He left and divorced his wife in order to marry Kathryn. He knew it. Kathryn knew it. He tried to tell people he had good, justifiable reasons for the divorce. Even as friends came around them, begging him not to divorce his wife, begging them not to marry, they were lost in their love for each other.

And their dream to serve Jesus Christ together.

They were married for six years.

Until one late Saturday afternoon, Kathryn left their apartment in the suburbs of Los Angeles and went for a walk. Down one tree-lined street after another. Passing home after home. Lost in thought, troubled in heart, knowing the weight of sin pressing down on her so hard it hurt deep.

She loved him.

With that, she looked up and saw what she didn't want to see. A simple street sign with two words piercing her heart.

Dead End.

"I had to make a choice," she said. "Would I serve the man I loved, or the God I loved? . . . For I loved him more than I loved life itself. And for a time, I loved him even more than God. . . . I said it out loud, 'Dear Jesus, I surrender all. I give it all to You. Take my body. Take my heart. All I am is yours. I place it in Your wonderful hands.'"[1]

Three days later, she was at the train station with her husband at her side. She held in her hand a one-way ticket to Franklin, Pennsylvania. "If you get on that train," he said softly, "you'll never see me again. . . . I will never interfere with your life or your ministry."[2]

And he kept his promise. Kathryn got on the train in 1944 because it was the right thing to do. For both of them. They couldn't keep on living a lie. Jesus Christ had been first in their lives, but somehow their hearts had shifted. She loved him. More than life itself.

On that Saturday afternoon, standing in front of the dead end sign, Kathryn knew that the time of testing had come. Jesus Christ now stood between her and her husband. Where He belonged.

And she made the choice. The choice we all have to make: Is Jesus Christ first in my life? Does He stand between me and everything?

Abraham, your son, your only son.

Had his heart shifted? Had he somehow made the gift of this miracle son bigger and a thousand times more than the Lord, the giver of his son? Did he do what we so often do, like little children refusing to share, clutching a gift given to us in our greedy little hands saying, "Mine! Mine!"? And the moment our parents see us, step in, and take it back, we immediately scream, "No! Mine! You can't have it!"

And our hearts shift.

It's a fact of life. There comes a time of testing. It always comes, right up to the point of our death, when the Lord demands our all. He stands between us and everything. First, always first. Heart, mind, and soul.

Where is your heart?

We are given a choice. We can choose to hold on, turn away, and say, "No, mine!" and pretend the time of testing has not come when, in fact, it has. Or we can choose to do what Kathryn did and say, "Dear Jesus, I surrender all." As Abraham did when he yielded his son back to the Lord.

Testing always comes with a choice. For Kathryn, that choice led to a lifetime of serving her Lord faithfully till the day she died. She got to do what she loved—tell people about Jesus. But it came, as it always comes, with great personal cost.

In February of 1970, twenty-six years after she boarded the train in Los Angeles, Kathryn received a Valentine's Day card in the mail. It was the first time he had written. And it was the last. Before he signed his name, he wrote on the card one word that said it all: *Love*.

She held the card and cried.

As Christ stood between.

QUESTIONS FOR REFLECTION

It's the hardest thing to know — when our heart shifts. We might see it in others. But why can't we see it in ourselves?

Is there anything in your life standing between you and the Lord?

NOTES

1. Jamie Buckingham, *Daughter of Destiny: The Authorized Biography of Kathryn Kuhlman* (Alachua, Fla.: Bridge-Logos, 1999), 94–95.

2. Ibid., 98.

36

DO WHAT YOU KNOW TO DO

Reflections on Genesis 22:1–4

*So Abraham rose early in the morning and saddled his
donkey, and took two of his young men with him and
Isaac his son; and he split wood for the burnt offering, and
arose and went to the place of which God had told him.*

—GENESIS 22:3

He knew what to do.

The Lord had spoken to Abraham: Go, take, offer. He didn't explain why. He didn't leave room for conversation. He spoke and that was that.

"Your son, your only son, whom you love" (Gen. 22:2).

Abraham was given a choice. Does he do it or not? Does he fudge? Maybe take time, a few days, a week, a month to consider what's being asked of him? Does he share the news with Sarah? Does he gather friends around him to talk about it? Does he do part but not all? Does he reinterpret? Does he think, "Maybe He meant a spiritual offering, not physical"?

At some point, Abraham made his decision. He chose to go. And at some point, on the journey, we know Abraham found the ability, the strength—the faith—to do what was being asked of him.

The New Testament tells us that. It says that faith came to Abraham. Real faith—faith that enabled him to walk straight into the time of testing. "By faith, Abraham, when he was tested, offered up Isaac" (Heb. 11:17).

But the question we don't know is this: When did he get that faith?

Is it possible it wasn't there when he woke up the next morning and did what he did because he knew he had to do what God wanted him to do? Because obedience is right; it's always right. Regardless of how he felt, whether he understood what was being asked of him, or whether he'd gotten the gift of faith or not. Is it possible?

What if Abraham woke the next morning "and saddled his donkey, and took two of his young men with him and Isaac his son; and he split wood for the burnt offering, and arose and went to the place of which God had told him" (Gen. 22:3), but didn't have that Hebrews 11:17 faith yet?

What if he was already grieving the death of his son? What if he couldn't bear the thought of making his son an offering—death at his own hand? How does he face life without Isaac? How does he come home and face Sarah? His family? His community? What if Abraham woke up and didn't want to do it?

What if he was doing what he was doing because he knew he had to? Because obedience is right; it's always right, because God is God and we are His servants. We do His will because we love Him. Even when we don't understand. Still, we say yes. Always yes. The Bible doesn't tell us the exact moment the Hebrews 11:17 faith came to

Abraham. But it does tell us that there isn't always a perfect order. Sometimes there is. Sometimes faith comes at the time of testing. It's there when we get the news our child has been rushed to the hospital, when we learn we've just lost our job, or when we suddenly find ourselves over-whelmed by circumstances—and can't cope. Faith is there. Faith to step straight into the story.

But other times, it's not there. We have to step out. We have to do what we have to do and trust that when we get there, the Lord Jesus Christ will meet us. Faith will come. Just obey. Just do what we know to do and trust that faith will follow.

Not easy. Never easy.

I remember being at the airport one late Thursday night. It was our first trip to Africa. We'd taken a flight to Europe and were waiting in the London airport for the flight to Kampala, Uganda. I don't know why it happened, but sud-denly I didn't want to go. I was afraid.

We were headed into a rural village hours away from the capital city. Away from hospitals, hotels, phones, and police. So if anything went wrong, we'd have no way out.

I was told the people suffered from extreme poverty. They walked miles just to get dirty water that had to be boiled to drink. When rebels came and attacked them, they died. When disease came, they died.

I suddenly didn't want to die.

Why did we say yes to our friends when they invited us to come? We'd met them in the US as they studied at seminary. We became friends. Close friends. We actually couldn't wait to see them again. We loved every moment of preparing for the trip.

But that was gone now.

Standing there, in the airport, I could feel the fear coursing through my veins. Making my heart beat fast, my hands sweat cold. Like if I got on that plane, I wasn't going to make it home. I wanted to turn and run through the concourse, find a hotel for the night, and fly back to the US in the morning. But I stood there . . . frozen. I knew I had to board. I knew I couldn't turn back. I had to do what I knew to do—when I didn't want to do it. Faith had vanished from my heart and fear came roaring in its place.

On the plane that night, my mind wandered back to a young man in our church who'd been diagnosed with cancer. The weeks in front him—chemo, radiation, surgery—were too much for him to bear.

I remembered the look in his eyes. Fear, terrifying fear.

For him, there were no choices. No ability to say, "No! I'm not doing this," and then turn and run wildly back into life as if it never happened. This young man had to take first steps. If he had any chance to survive, he knew he had no choice.

So he did what he knew to do and trusted the Lord would meet him there.

And He did. Just as He promises. Faith did come. Faith and ability and strength to handle the days—sometimes the hours—in front of him. Oh, there were times, many times, fear came back. Faith fled like a deer spooked in the woods, and he cried out for help. But right up to the end, before he died a few months later, faith was stronger than fear. He knew Jesus was with him. He knew peace from the Lord in his heart. We saw it. All of us did, as we witnessed the grace of the Lord Jesus Christ shining through his beautiful face.

In his story, obedience came first. Obedience filled with fear. Faith followed.

Maybe it was the same for Abraham. Maybe, just maybe, he said to himself, "Just take the boy, Abraham. Just take the boy and go. Trust the Lord will meet you on the mountain."

And for me, well, I had to do the same thing. I had to tell myself, "Just get on the plane, Barnum. Just do it. With heart pounding. With sweat on your forehead. With fear gripping your insides. Just do it."

Because that's the way it is sometimes. We just do what we know to do.

And trust that faith will come.

QUESTIONS FOR REFLECTION

Philippians 4:13 says we can do all things through Christ who strengthens us. I can't imagine going through life's testing alone. We need the Lord in it. Have you ever asked for faith to come? Faith for all you have to face?

The hardest piece is saying yes to God. Yes when we don't understand why have to go through what's in front of us. But can you say it, knowing He is good, right, holy, true, and trustworthy?

37

GLIMPSES

~✌~

Reflections on Genesis 22:5–6

> *Abraham said to his young men, "Stay here with the*
> *donkey, and I and the lad will go over there;*
> *and we will worship and return to you."*

—Genesis 22:5

When faith comes, you know what you didn't know before. You see what you couldn't see before.

By the third day, Abraham had a glimpse.

A few days earlier, the Lord had told Abraham to go to Moriah and do the unthinkable—to offer his son as a sacrificial offering. How was it possible? How could he do what only pagan religions do? What was the Lord thinking? Why did He want his son? Abraham didn't know why. Nor did he ask. He just did it. He got up the next morning, packed up, got his son Isaac, two of his young men, wood for the offering, and set out for Moriah.

One foot in front of the other.

Because that's what we do. We obey Him. We do what He has told us to do even when we don't understand. One foot in front of the other, trusting Him. Trusting He will meet us on the road ahead. Somehow. Somewhere.

Because—in Abraham's past—He always had.

When the Lord told Abraham to leave his homeland and go, he did. Trusting the Lord. Trusting Him to lead. When he was told he'd have a son, the Lord gave him faith to see. Faith to believe. Just enough. But not enough for him to see everything. Not the particulars. Which is why Ishmael came first. Abraham and Sarah didn't see the whole story. They didn't fully understand the Lord intended the promised son to come from Sarah (see Gen. 16:1–6).

And sometimes faith is like that. It comes in stages. We see a little. But not the whole.

Like a friend of mine.

"It's been a hard, painful year," he told me. "When I became senior pastor ten months ago, I was told the church was healthy in every respect. We accepted the call to come based on what we were told. And none of it was true."

I could see the anguish and betrayal written deep in his face.

"My wife and I were so happy where we were before. When I got the first invitation to be considered for this church, I turned it down. We weren't interested. But there was a nagging inside I couldn't get rid of. So my wife and I called wise, trusted friends to come alongside and meet with us. Pray with us. And that's what we did. Eventually, we believed the Lord made it clear that we were to come here and serve these people. We were sure of it."

Two weeks on the job and it all came crashing down.

"It was like finding out your new house is infested with termites. Of course, everything looks great on the outside. But the inside? It's all rot." He said that as soon as he learned the real story, he wanted to leave. Grab his wife and kids, pack up and get out of town. They felt they had made the biggest mistake of their lives.

"It kept getting worse," he went on. "Multiple scandals. Mismanaged money. Unpaid bills. Unmet loans. I was told the church had cash reserves and was fiscally sound when, in fact, I come to find out there's debt. Sizeable debt. Insurmountable debt. At the same time—get this—the church has an image in the community of being vibrant, healthy, active in mission, and alive in Christ!"

He shook his head in disbelief. He chose not to speak ill about the former pastor, but he did talk about issues of corruption, greed, pride, and the insatiable lust of a church family wanting to make a name for themselves locally and nationally.

"I didn't agree to come and deal with this—not this," he said quietly. Sadly.

"What are you going to do?" I inquired.

"One foot in front of the other," he said, and then he smiled. "About two weeks ago, my wife and I were really in bad shape. We were almost at the point of resigning. That night, I found myself wrestling with the Lord in prayer. I was begging Him to help me. I've never felt so beaten down in all my life. And that night I went to bed and—surprisingly— slept peacefully through the night. When I woke up, I knew something was different. Something I wasn't expecting."

"What's that?" I asked.

"I got a glimpse. Just a glimpse of why we're here. It's like the Lord whispered in my ear in the middle of the night and said, 'Put this house in order.' When I woke up, I knew what I didn't know before. I could see what I couldn't see before. The Lord had called us here for a purpose. I turned to my wife and said, 'Guess what? The Lord sent us here for a purpose!'" He smiled again and said, "I have no idea how to bring order in the midst of this unbelievable mess. But I know it's going to come. Yes I do."

Glimpses.

One foot in front of the other.

That may be exactly what happened to Abraham as he approached Moriah. Out of his mouth came the unexpected, the miraculous. He turned to his young men and told them to wait. "Stay here with the donkey, and I and the lad will go over there; and we will worship and return to you" (Gen. 22:5).

He was about to do what the Lord had told him to do. To offer his son. And yet, at the same time, Abraham knew more. Saw more. And he spoke it in the tiny word: *we*. He said, "We will return to you."

Abraham will return . . . with his son. How is that possible? That can't be. Unless the Lord had whispered in Abraham's ear. Maybe not the details. Maybe not the particulars. But enough to see a little. Just enough to catch the smallest glimpse.

And sometimes faith is like that.

QUESTIONS FOR REFLECTION

There is profound truth in putting one foot in front of the other. Sometimes we don't move until we get the glimpse, not realizing it will come as we move. Do you put one foot in front of the other, expecting faith to come as you go?

There is a prayer that says, "Lord, show us just enough. Not too much that we can't bear it. Not too little that we get lost and confused. But enough to walk in faith today." Do you pray for enough? Faith enough to do what He is calling you to do?

38

SEEING BIG

Reflections on Genesis 22:6–10

Isaac spoke to Abraham his father and said, "My father!"
And he said, "Here I am, my son." And he said, "Behold, the
fire and the wood, but where is the lamb for the burnt offering?"
Abraham said, "God will provide for Himself the lamb for the
burnt offering, my son." So the two of them walked on together.

—GENESIS 22:7–8

He bound his son. He laid him on the altar. He took the knife. He stretched out his hand.

The Bible records nothing here. No sounds. Was Isaac screaming? Was Abraham screaming back? No prayers. No last minute negotiations. No hesitation or change of mind. No expression of face. No tears. No sign of terror. Nothing but the act itself.

The arm in motion. Seconds before the knife plunged into the chest of his son. Abraham saw big.

That's what the Bible tells us. It was more, so much more, than cold obedience. The kind where God speaks, we obey and that's that. Whether we understand it or not. Whether we want to do it or not. As if it all bypasses the heart.

This was different. The Lord met Abraham as he went. We see it at the base of the mountain when Abraham saw a glimpse of the story. He turned to his young men and told them that both he and his son would return. Both of them (see Gen. 22:5).

We see it again when Isaac suddenly asked his father, "Where is the lamb for the burnt offering?" And Abraham responded, "God will provide for Himself the lamb for the burnt offering, my son" (Gen. 22:7–8).

Abraham saw big.

He knew something was going to happen. Something of God. He didn't know what. He didn't know how. But he knew. The Bible tells us that. "By faith Abraham . . . considered that God is able to raise people even from the dead" (Heb. 11:17, 19).

So even if Isaac died, the Lord has power to make him live. Power even to raise from the dead. Abraham saw that. He had glimpses that kept getting bigger. Fuller.

Faith is like that. It has eyes to see God working in the present. But it can be more. Sometimes it's as if a door in heaven opens and we—just for a quick moment—get to see in. See big. See beyond the present time. See what God is doing now and what He's going to do in the days to come.

This is what happened to the prophets. They saw ahead. They saw the coming of Messiah. His suffering. His glory to follow.

Abraham had a taste of that. He had, as the Bible says about faith, "the conviction of things not seen" (Heb. 11:1). On the mount of Moriah, Abraham had eyes to see. He believed in the God of resurrection. Does that sound crazy?

It happened to Becca, on her deathbed in the hospital. Her husband Tim at her bedside. And the door of heaven flew open. She saw, but Tim couldn't. He had his hand resting on her arm, praying. Praying the Lord would heal her. Praying with tears, crying from the anguish of his soul, for God to do the impossible.

"I need you to stop praying that," she stated emphatically. "Can't you see? The angels are here. The Lord is calling me home. You need to let me go."

Tim looked up at her. He said later that, at first, he thought it was the sickness talking. Or the drugs. She'd been in and out of consciousness.

"Let me go, sweetheart," she said quietly. "Let me go."

Somehow, at that moment, Tim saw that she could see what he couldn't. This was faith talking. Not the sickness. Not the drugs. The Lord had done this and she was ready when he wasn't. And he told her so.

"I can't. I don't want to. You need to stay."

But Becca saw big. Her hand now in his. But her eyes focused, still looking through the door.

It doesn't make sense for those of us who can't see. A friend of mine told me it's like looking at the backside of a hand-woven rug. It's all a complicated confused mess of knots and material that reveal no pattern. No artistry. No beauty. Not until you look at the front side and suddenly it all comes together. Everything in its perfect place. Its perfect order.

And the door opens. For just a moment, we can see big.

I wonder how much Abraham could see. Did he know that one day, at the very place he was standing on Mount Moriah, that King Solomon would build the Lord's temple? And that it would be here where Israel would come to worship and sacrifice their lambs for the burnt offerings? Same exact place (see 2 Chron. 3:1).

Did he know that one day the Messiah would stand here too? Remember, Abraham saw big. Jesus told us that. He said, "Abraham rejoiced to see My day, and he saw it, and was glad" (John 8:56).

But how much did he see? How wide had the door opened? He saw big enough to believe in the God who is able to raise the dead. Big enough, as his hand clutched the knife and began its downward motion to pierce the heart of his son, to believe the Lord was in command. And it was right to obey Him.

It's what we do.

But could he see bigger? A thousand times bigger? That one day there would be another father, the Father Himself, who would do what he was doing. This act of offering His Son. And that His Son would be what Isaac could never be.

The real Lamb for the burnt offering. No, not Isaac. Another Isaac, the Messiah to come. And for this reason, the Lord shouted to Abraham. "'Abraham, Abraham!' And he said, 'Here I am.' He said, 'Do not stretch out your hand against the lad, and do nothing to him; for now I know that you fear God, since you have not withheld your son, your only son, from Me'" (Gen. 22:11–12).

And for just a moment, the door opened so wide, so big, that maybe, just maybe, Abraham could see the wonder, the glories, the mystery of the ages to come.

The Father. His Son, His only Son. Offered for us all.

QUESTIONS FOR REFLECTION

Hebrews 11:10, 13–16 tells us Abraham saw the city of God yet to come and longed for it. Too often we pray small, ask small, and see small. Is there something inside you that longs to see big? Bigger than here? Bigger to what God has promised you to come?

Sometimes people have visions that are not of God, not attested to by Scripture. It always needs to be tested by the church so we don't fall into confusion. But when God does it—when He gives faith to your heart—do you know it? Can you feel it encourage you in heart, mind, and soul?

39
CHRIST STANDING BETWEEN

Reflections on Genesis 22:11–19

But the angel of the L*ORD called to him from heaven and said, "Abraham, Abraham!" And he said, "Here I am."*

—Genesis 22:11

And the preacher in the pulpit said, "Lay down your Isaac!"

Marvelous sermon. Easier said than done. Or as the old expression goes, "Been there. Done that." Because most of us know the story. We do everything we're supposed to do. We go through all the right steps. And just when we think we're free and the idol of our heart is finally smashed, it's back.

So we do it again. And again. Until there is this massive disconnect between what we're being told to do and what's real. Eventually, we learn to tune it out.

But the fact is, idols are all too real. Idols sneak into our hearts. Good ones. Bad ones. Outrageously fun ones. Cunning, sly, wickedly deceiving ones we don't know, or don't admit we know, until something or someone tries to take it from us. We react and the strength of our reaction tells us all we need to know.

We have idols rooted deep in our soul.

Good ones with people we love. Bad ones with addictions that we once controlled but now control us. Fun ones with things we do, places we go, social circles we travel in, that fill us with an intoxicating pleasure we can't imagine living without. Deceiving ones, the worst of which is in the mirror. Somehow, somewhere along the way, we actually believe our own press.

We have idols.

We don't tend to do anything about it. Not until we have to. Not until someone loves us enough to tell us. Or maybe one day we wake up and realize that something other than God is god of us. And we can't go on like that.

Lay down your Isaac!

And we try. And try. And try again. To take our hands off the ones we love and give them to the Lord. To push our addictions away. To enforce self-control in areas of excessive pleasure. To see ourselves rightly before God.

And it works, a little. For a while. Maybe, for some of us, during the season of Lent.

It's here, right here, where the church has often been so utterly powerless. The gospel we preach is often devoid of anything supernatural and miraculous. As if, somehow, by enforcing certain disciplines for us to do we will overcome the tyranny of the gods that plague our lives and we will be free.

It's simple: Just do it. Know what your Isaac is. Then lay it down.

Of course, this is not what happened to Abraham in the actual story. He didn't wake up one morning and think to himself he had a problem with Isaac. That his love for his son had become greater than his love for the Lord.

God did that.

God stepped in. He spoke to Abraham. He did the work all by Himself. He put his finger on Abraham's heart and demanded three things: his son Isaac, full and uncompromised obedience, and finally, most importantly, worship. Worship on the mountain. Worship with a sacrificial offering. Worship as God designed it from before time began.

What could Abraham do? He could obey. What couldn't he do? He couldn't take the idol from his heart. None of us can.

This is the greatest deception possible. And most of us fall for it. We believe we have the power and ability first to identify, and second to dethrone the gods that take first place in our heart. It's a lie; we can't.

This is the work of God alone. And He makes it strikingly clear as to how it's done through this story. He called Abraham to Mount Moriah to worship Him. This must always be our starting point. We come before God. We put our eyes, our heart, our full attention on Him. We praise Him. We give Him thanks. We ask Him to reveal our idols, and when He does, we bind them. We lay them on the altar. We take the knife and do what we need to do to offer them to the Lord. But that's it. All we can do now is to raise our hands. Surrender our heart. Focus body, mind, and soul upon the Lord.

And then wait. Wait for Him to make the transaction. Wait for His power to do the work. To set us free. Real power flooding our souls, forgiving our sins, removing the idols—like a surgeon removing a deadly cancer. And then replacing it with the one and only thing our heart was perfectly designed for.

Him. Only Him.

It's what He does.

He calls us to come, worship, and lay down our idols. He provides the perfect sacrifice for the forgiveness of our sins. And then He does what we need Him to do.

Sometimes it happens in a moment. Sometimes it's a process and happens over time. Either way, the Lord does the work. He changes the heart. He puts things in order. Everything in its proper place. And when He does, the idols cease to be the idols. The Lord takes His rightful place in our heart and it's over. We know it. We know it real and deep in our soul.

Dietrich Bonhoeffer said it perfectly: "The tables are completely turned, Abraham receives Isaac back, but henceforth he will have his son in quite a new way. . . . Abraham comes down from the mountain with Isaac just as he went up, but the whole situation has changed. Christ has stepped between father and son. . . . Outwardly the picture is unchanged, but the old is passed away, and behold all things are new."[1]

What powerful imagery—Abraham and Isaac coming down the mountain with Christ standing between them. Everything forever changed.

A new Abraham. A new perspective. A new heart.

Christ standing between.

QUESTIONS FOR REFLECTION

Can you see that in your life? Christ standing between you and what you love most?

Without thinking about it, we often come to worship the Lord with our idols. We want both. We want the Lord to allow us both. But does He? Is it possible for you to let Him have your Isaacs? Are you willing to call on His name and ask Him to do what you can't?

NOTE

1. Dietrich Bonhoeffer, *The Cost of Discipleship* (New York: Touchstone, 1995), 99.

40

IT'S WHAT WE DO

Reflections on Genesis 22:15–19

And your offspring shall possess the gate of his enemies,
and in your offspring shall all the nations of the earth
be blessed, because you have obeyed my voice.

—GENESIS 22:17–18 ESV

Rich stared out his office window, nervous, thinking, "What have I done?"

He could hear people gathering outside his office. In just a few minutes, he'd grab the letter on his desk and join them. He'd do the small talk. Call the meeting to order. Then drop the bomb.

He didn't have to do this. No one was expecting it. He could postpone, again. In one sense, he should have done this two months ago. Then again three weeks ago. But he reasoned himself out of it. Said he needed time to pray. Time with his wife. Time to put off what he knew he had to do: resign.

Resign because his boss messed up. Messed up big. Doing what should never have been done. Immoral. Unethical. The list seemed endless. The biggest: He stole funds. He took designated money and redirected them for political favor.

A politician at heart, changing policy and undermining core principles.

"When you lose core principles," Rich taught endlessly, "you lose yourself." And that's exactly what was happening. Which forced him to confront his boss. Not publicly, not to embarrass him; but quietly; strongly, even compassionately.

"You're either with me," his boss resisted, "or you're not. Which is it?"

Time. He needed time. He should have spoken out. Made his stand, right then, but he didn't. He kicks himself now. But he was too scared, too unsure.

Two kids in college. One not far behind. No job prospects. No paycheck. No home because he lived in company housing. And all of it ends the moment he resigns. The letter was in his hand. The people gathered in the other room.

"What have I done? What am I doing?"

If only this was business. Maybe it wouldn't hurt so much. Maybe he'd even be treated better. Severance. Mercy. But this was the *church*. His boss, the bishop. An ungodly man who had put his hand to sign documents that boldly, defiantly denied key doctrines of the historic Christian faith founded in Christ Jesus our Lord.

"Come against Him," he finally had the courage to tell the bishop, "you come against me."

But the bishop just laughed. "You swore at your ordination to obey your bishop. Now your church owes us money. Write the check or I'll remove you from office. Because I can."

But he won't. Not now. He won't have to. Not with the letter in his hand.

It was time.

He went into the meeting with his church elders and resigned. He took the step, the big step, off the cliff, because it's what we do. What we always do. And it's what he taught, a thousand times taught: Lose your core principles and you lose yourself. And no core principle ran deeper than his love for the Lord.

"We obey Him first," Rich told his elders, "then those in authority over us. That's the order. If those in authority over us deny Him, we can't stand idly by. We must speak out. We can't follow them. To do that is to condone their actions. And I can't. I won't. We obey the Lord. It's what we do. And we do it because we love Him. Just as Jesus obeyed His Father because He loved Him. Remember His words: 'That the world may know that I love the Father, I do exactly as the Father commanded Me'" (John 14:31).

With that, he handed them his resignation. The deed was done.

But what happened next surprised him. He had forgotten the old biblical principle that blessing always follows obedience.

"Because you have obeyed My voice," the Lord said to Abraham. "I will greatly bless you, and I will greatly multiply your seed as the stars of the heavens and as the sand which is on the seashore; and your seed shall possess the gate of their enemies. In your seed all the nations of the earth shall be blessed, because you have obeyed My voice" (Gen. 22:17–18).

Sounds right. Sounds great. Until you actually have to do it. Until you have to march up your own Mount Moriah.

Until you have to sign your name to the resignation letter. And then wake up the next day with no job. No home. No idea where the next paycheck is coming from to provide for your family.

"I'll go with you," said one of the elders.

"Me too" said another. "Count me in."

Eight of the ten immediately resigned with him. "We'll go with you. We'll help you get a new home. We'll find a place to meet on Sunday mornings. We'll bless those who want to stay with the church and bless those who want to go. But you're not doing this alone. We get to make this stand for Jesus with you."

With that, the ten of them talked and made a decision with one voice. Even the two who opposed agreed to the proposal.

"You know we don't have much money," one of them said. "But we will do everything we can to raise at least three months' severance to help you and your family."

Someone seconded the motion. And it passed, just like that.

Rich was stunned. "I don't know what to say. Thank you. But are you sure? The bishop will not be happy with your decision tonight. He will do everything in his power to convince this church to come against me. You know that, don't you? Perhaps you should reconsider."

One of the two who decided to stay with the church chuckled and spoke up. "We've done what's right tonight. Just like you. And we'll tell him what you told us. We have to obey the Lord first. It's our core principle!"

Because it's what we do. It's what we always do.

QUESTIONS FOR REFLECTION

Finding identity is finding the Lord at the center of our lives. Lose Him and we lose everything. Every once in a while, we're faced with situations of compromise. We have to stand up, speak out, and take risks. Do you know this story in your life? Times of compromise? Times of taking a stand?

With obedience comes blessing. Sometimes blessing comes immediately. Sometimes suffering comes first, and we don't see the blessing right away. But the principle — do you believe it's true? Is it something you can tightly hold on to as you do what's right in your life?

PART 6

CONFLICT
IN JESUS

41

THE SPIN CYCLE

Reflections on Exodus 32:1–6

The people assembled about Aaron and said to him,
"Come, make us a god who will go before us; as for this
Moses, the man who brought us up from the land of Egypt,
we do not know what has become of him."

—EXODUS 32:1

I don't remember signing up for the game. But suddenly I find myself caught in it. I'm spinning in this guy's crazy mess and stupid enough to really think the mess is mine.

He's a friend. A mentor. Older in the Lord. Someone to respect.

One minute I'm more than just a friend. I'm his best friend. Confidant. Closer than close. The next minute I don't measure up. Like I've said something wrong. Done something wrong. Like I've broken trust.

I feel him push me away.

Sometimes it's subtle. So subtle I find myself going over the conversations in my mind and wondering if he meant what he said. Or was he being sarcastic? I don't know. I can't tell if I'm being valued or put down. On the inner circle or the outer circle. And why do I care so much? Why do I think about it so much?

Spin. Spin.

Other times he does it publically. In front of my colleagues. One minute the praise. The next minute the jab. The put-down. The sarcasm at my expense. Like I don't fit it. Don't make the grade. Just not good enough.

I don't know how it happened. Or when it happened. But a day came when everything in my life seemed to revolve around him. His moods. His standard of right and wrong. Acceptable. Not acceptable. Inside. Outside. Favored. Not favored. The definition of being cool or being a big fat joke. Outcast one day. Adored the next. Then back again.

Spin. Spin. Did I sign up for this?

Here's what's even crazier. Without even knowing it, I'm in his orbit. Caught in this massive gravitational force. Pulled and jerked. Suddenly needing one thing from him—just one thing—I've got to make sure I'm on his good side. Today. Every day. On the in. Always on the in.

Exhausting.

Breaking the orbit isn't easy. For me, it started with a simple phrase. The first commandment: "You shall have no other gods before Me" (Ex. 20:3). The Lord wanted me in His orbit. Not someone else's. Not just in theory or in principle. But in real daily practice. My mind. My heart. My emotions.

I had no idea how to do that practically.

Up to that point, I only knew of two options. I either spin in this guy's orbit and do my best to be the best in his eyes, or I rebel. Pull away, break away. Act like I don't care. Which only provokes heated confrontations. And who wants that? It's easier to give in.

And spin.

In a profound way, I understand Aaron, Moses' brother. When Moses went up Mount Sinai for forty days, Aaron found himself in the middle of politics. In the people's spin. They wanted, needed, and demanded the gods of their past. And they needed Aaron to be the man to lead them.

But Aaron knew better. He knew the first commandment. He also knew and experienced the first principle of sin. We need someone, something to control us. Doesn't matter that it never worked in the past. We forget the gods we once served failed us. They didn't satisfy. They didn't deliver us from the bondage, slavery, and oppression of our captors.

We *need* to spin. We *want* to spin.

Even when we know the cruelty of it all. The pain that sears the soul.

And Aaron gave in. That's what politics does. It pleases the people. It climbs into their orbit of crazed control. Then, like magic, the leader becomes the one around whom that tiny little world spins. Both spinning each other. In a broken, messed-up world of hyper-dysfunction.

The Bible calls it the golden calf. But, to be honest, it's really the face of the one we're spinning around.

Aaron did what should never have been done. Instead of having no other gods before God, Aaron did the exact opposite. He took the newly made golden calf and put it right in front of the Lord's altar.

The calf. The Lord's altar. Both together.

I get that. For the longest time, I spun in this guy's orbit believing the Lord was in it. Like it was God's will and plan for my life to let this man, this elder statesman—for me, one of my golden calves—spin me. Control me.

Like I said, I don't remember signing up for the game. But I do remember the Lord's kindness in getting me out.

There came a day when it was over. I acknowledged my sin in allowing myself to get caught. I also confessed I didn't have the ability to break the orbit myself. Even when I tried, I was still reacting to this man's reactions.

But the Lord did what I couldn't do, and when He did it, it was really, really over.

It's not like I left the relationship. I didn't. It's just that he couldn't control me anymore. He couldn't push my buttons and make me spin in his spin. Oh, how he tried. But the power was gone. The gravitational force of the spin no longer had an effect on me. His mess was no longer my mess.

And I was free. Free to worship the Lord. Free to be in this man's company. Free to love him and serve him as Jesus has loved and served me. Free not to react to all his sharp jabs. The put-downs. The sarcasm or the praise. Free to be on the inside or the outside. It didn't matter anymore because I was spinning in the only orbit worth spinning in.

QUESTIONS FOR REFLECTION

Will you take the first commandment test? Do you have others gods in your life? Any golden calves?

Without Jesus Christ, it is impossible to see — let alone break — the relational dysfunctions that have plagued some of us from our earliest days. We spin, and it's normal to us. Do you spin? Do you want Him in your life to help you see — and break — the spin?

42

CRASH AND BURN

Reflections on Exodus 32:7–20

Then the LORD spoke to Moses, "Go down at once,
for your people, whom you brought up from the land
of Egypt, have corrupted themselves."

—EXODUS 32:7

The pastor daydreams at his desk.

In his hand, a ticket out. Tomorrow morning he gets on a plane. Goes for an interview. Bigger church. New start.

He is *so* done.

The politics at church are stifling. Friends, even good friends, are cornering him. Complaining. Something's always wrong with him, his preaching, his leadership style. He's just not pleasing enough of the people enough of the time.

He wants out.

He understands Aaron. It's like he can preach the gospel as long as the people don't have to give up the gods of the American culture: self-indulgence, self-gratification, self-promotion. Always enflaming the lusts of self at the center. It's like he hears the cry, "Give us Jesus! Teach the Bible. But the golden calves we worship stay."

He dreams. A bigger church. Bigger staff. Bigger platform to impact the world. He's always had that dream. His wife whispers in his ear. She's willing to go. But she asks, "Are we hearing God's call or running from it?" But he's already gone. His heart is somewhere else. Dreaming big. Having no idea his dreams are filled with self—a golden calf with a face just like his.

A woman on the elder board makes an appointment to see him. She knows what's going on without being told. She begs him to stay. She's gone before the Lord in prayer. She has three things she wants to tell him. The first is the most important: "Shepherds stay. They don't run. They give themselves completely for the flock. They lay down their lives because they love. Really love. Please, love us enough to stay."

The second thing: "It's not going to be different somewhere else. You know that, right?" She's not sure why it isn't obvious. The Bible says it plainly. It happens here. It happens everywhere. Wolves torment the church. From the inside. From the outside. Causing division. Denying the faith. Shepherds know that. Surely pastors do too, right?

But there's one more thing to say. The hardest of the three. She has to say it but she doesn't want to. She's afraid of his reaction. Afraid it will hurt him. Afraid he won't take it the right way and maybe it will hurt their relationship: "It's a real temptation for pastors, isn't it? Being looked at by a bigger church. Being wanted somewhere else. I bet it's hard to say no."

Then she stopped. She wanted to go on. She wanted to use his own words from his own sermons. "Like you always say, 'Self at the center! Self that rules our culture. Rules our hearts. When will Jesus Christ be the center of our lives? When will He be enough for us?'" But she doesn't. And she wonders if she has said enough.

He doesn't let her see his reaction. Everything stays polite. He thanks her for coming. For praying. For speaking her heart. He tells her it meant so much.

But he hears the sound of the crash. Deep inside the story of the golden calf, there is a moment when Moses takes the stone tablets in his hand and throws them down at the foot of the mountain. Shattered into pieces. The breaking of God's Word. "It came about, as soon as Moses came near the camp, that he saw the calf and the dancing; and Moses' anger burned, and he threw the tablets from his hands and shattered them at the foot of the mountain" (Ex. 32:19). Or was it the other sound of the golden calf crashing into flames? "He took the calf which they had made and burned it with fire, and ground it to powder, and scattered it over the surface of the water and made the sons of Israel drink it" (Ex. 32:20).

For just a moment, he sees his own sin. His own golden calf. For just a moment, he hears the crash and burn. It's what happens to idols. All idols. Crash. Burn. And then Moses made them drink the calf, ground to dust, mixed in water. Poison to the body. Poison to the soul.

A communion of death.

For just a moment, this woman became to him like a little Moses. Her voice almost the same as his wife's: "Are we hearing God's call or running from it?"

And he got it. He really got it.

And then he didn't.

The ticket was still in his hand. All he had to do was make a few calls and cancel the trip. Say no. Not interested. And stay the course.

But the daydreams came back strong, too strong. The possibilities of what might be. The sheer joy of getting out of the old. Going someplace new. And not just new. Big.

And that's exactly what he did. He got the job. Moved his family. Left the old church he served for so many years without regret. Without looking back. Without knowing the hurt he left in his wake.

No idea, in all the thrill of new and big, that self was still reigning at the center. That silly little golden calf. No idea that what happened before will happen again. And because of it, another Moses will knock on his door, look him in the eyes, and do what all Moseses do. They shatter tablets. They turn our idols into flames.

Crash. Burn. Drink.

So that we might choose life.

QUESTIONS FOR REFLECTION

Every once in a while, we get a glimpse of our idols. Our Moses comes and we're given a choice. What do you know about this—the choice for your idols to crash and burn? Or the choice for the idols to stay?

How do we become a Moses to people in need? How do we let others help us get the log out of our eyes so we can be helpful to those suffering with specks in theirs (see Matt. 7:3–5)?

43

GOING DE-CALF

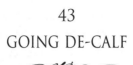

Reflections on Exodus 32:25–29

*Then Moses stood in the gate of the camp, and said,
"Whoever is for the LORD, come to me!" And all the
sons of Levi gathered together to him.*

—EXODUS 32:26

It's hard to break from culture.

Best to live for Christ with a little bit of culture. Or to
live for culture with a little bit of Christ. The two meshed
together like the golden calf in front of the altar.

And then party!

"The people sat down to eat and to drink, and rose up
to play" (Ex. 32:6). Just like today. A world at play. A
church—well, for a lot of us anyway—also at play.

Pastors caught between both worlds because, God forbid,
they challenge the freedom the culture now gives us. They'll
get instant pushback. Criticism for standing for the Bible
at those points the Bible doesn't stand for the culture.
They'll be mocked for being insensitive. Uncaring. Without
compassion. Judgmental. Worse if they call people to repent
of sins the culture no longer sees as sin. That will make
them feel like outcasts. Marginalized. Persecuted.

So we do church like we do halftime at a football game. Or intermission at the local bar when the band takes a break. We have our church services—doing what we do as Christians—and when we're done we go back to the game, back to the band, and rock.

A little bit of culture. A little bit of Christ.

She felt marginalized. Judged. Like the world around her has more compassion for her than Christians do.

She had been at the church for about a year. Her husband started coming a few months later. The more they came, the more they liked it and decided to get involved. First with a ministry to the poor in the city on Saturday afternoons, then every other week to hang out with Christians at a nearby home.

It just fit. Everything about the church fit.

One night, in conversation, she said it so casually. Like it was no big deal.

A woman asked her how long she'd been married. Her face lit up with surprise. "O my gosh, no, we're not married. We've lived together for about three years. We've talked about it some. But no, we're not ready for that."

"So how did you two meet?" the woman asked.

"In college. We dated for a while. Then after college, went our separate ways. Couple of years later, we met up and decided to try again. Give it some time. It's been great for both of us."

"I'm glad you found our church," the woman responded.

"We are too. He's from the south. He's got a strong Christian family. Grew up in the church from the day he was born. My family not so much. It really wasn't a big thing for me until I got to college. But now, I wouldn't dream of missing it and sometimes it feels like I'm dragging him here!"

She smiled, having no idea that two worlds clashed together into one.

There's nothing worse than Moses.

He comes down from Mount Sinai and completely trashes the golden calf. No dialogue. No church politics. No yearlong studies, massive position papers, well-publicized conferences to listen to both sides of the issue and then adopt a well-crafted, deeply sensitive resolution of semi-daring compromise.

Party over.

"Whoever is for the LORD, come to me!" (Ex. 32:26). He doesn't care who feels marginalized. Unheard. Uncared for. He doesn't care if the pastors and church leaders are divided over the issue. He doesn't care if he's stomped on people's rights to freely express themselves.

He cares about the glory of God.

That it's not about us first. It's about Him first. And when it's about Him first, it's actually about us too. The best for us. The Lord wants the best for us. But He will never compromise His glory. Never.

You can have culture. You can have Christ.

But when the two come into conflict, you can't have both. You have to choose.

The woman did it so well. She called her up, asked her to lunch, said she wanted to talk to her about something. Her new friend eagerly accepted the invite.

She did it with love. Compassion and mercy. Kindness and grace.

"It's hard to break from culture," she said. "Especially our culture where sexual freedom permeates everything. But there comes a time when it's right to follow Jesus Christ and do what He wants for our lives. And not just for us, but for our children after us."

She loved her enough to tell her the truth. About marriage. About living together. About what it means to want His best for her, her future husband, and their family.

"Marriage belongs to God," she said. "He takes the two and makes them one and when He does that, nothing can break it apart. But we have to do it His way and His way isn't the way of the culture around us."

Her friend listened. Smiled. Nodded at the appropriate times. But inside, anger was mounting. She felt judged. Wronged. Looked down on. Like she didn't fit into the perfect Christian image of this woman from her church.

"Is this what the pastors think too?" she asked. And when she heard her say, "Yes," she put her napkin on the table, stood up, and grabbed her purse.

"I can find a church that's not as rigid as yours," she said in disgust.

And she did.

With a little bit of culture. And a little bit of Christ.

QUESTIONS FOR REFLECTION

It's hard to talk about the culture around us. We're so much a part of it. Many feel today the Bible is just antiquated—outdated—and wrong about the moral issues of our times. But is it really? Has God changed? Or have we been caught between two worlds?

Our Lord wants our identity to be strong in Him. Strong enough to go into the culture, not to isolate from it, not to be entangled by it, but to be witnesses in love to it. Can you be in it and not compromise? Are you sure enough of who you are in the Lord?

44

I'M OUT

Reflections on Exodus 33:1–7

*Then the LORD spoke to Moses, "Depart, go up from here,
you and the people whom you have brought up from the
land of Egypt, to the land of which I swore to Abraham, Isaac,
and Jacob, saying, 'To your descendants I will give it.'"*

—EXODUS 33:1

He said He'd be with us. He said He'd dwell in our midst. He said He'd never leave us (see Ex. 25:8; 29:42–46; Lev. 26:11–12; Num. 2:2; 34:36; Deut. 31:6–8).

But the golden-calf story changed all that. Sin always does. It may be small in our eyes. But it's big in His. Serious big. Breaking, dividing, hurting, destroying the sacred bonds of love, trust, and compassion between us. Big.

And He was suddenly out.

"Go up to a land flowing with milk and honey; for I will not go up in your midst, because you are an obstinate people, and I might destroy you on the way" (Ex. 33:3).

Our sin, His holiness—they don't mix. People cringe at the thought that He'd ever leave us. Worse, that He'd destroy us. We don't see God that way. We don't want God that way. We want the understanding, caring, merciful God. The loving God.

The One who always stays. No matter what we do. Because sin just isn't that big to us. That serious. That costly. We want the One who'd never say, "I'm out."

I will remember her always. I tell her story nearly everywhere I go.

I found her after church at the café, sitting by herself. Such a regal woman. Distinguished. In her mid- to late eighties. I was the visiting preacher that day. I caught her eye and decided to go and sit with her.

"You know who I am, don't you" she asked me, her British accent like the queen of England. Her hand reaching out to touch my arm.

I told her I was sorry. I didn't know her name.

She told me she was the widow of a prominent Anglican theologian by the name of Philip Edgecombe Hughes, whose commentaries on Hebrews and 2 Corinthians are still among the very best.

"O dear lady," I said, a bit startled, "what are you doing at this church?" This wandering church.

They are Christians. They believe Jesus is Lord and Savior of their church. They believe the Bible is true. Their bishop did not. He laughed at the Bible. He publically called Jesus Christ a sinner like everyone else. He demanded that he be allowed to come to the church and preach his twisted gospel among them.

But they wouldn't let him. How could they?

So the bishop threatened to take their building—because he could. Their historic building. With a graveyard attached. He didn't have to threaten twice.

They left. All the history. All the memories. All the Lord did among them for decades upon decades in that church building. They left it all.

They became nomads.

Eventually, they found a new church home. And Mrs. Hughes went with them. She left that beautiful historic church building. And the graveyard.

And suddenly I understood. "What about your husband?" I asked, "Isn't he buried at the old church? Are you saying you left your husband behind?"

Mrs. Hughes had the brightest smile. She looked me straight in the eyes and said with profound, unforgettable wisdom, "Young man, I never promised to follow my husband's bones. I promised to follow his faith!"

I nodded. He would have done the same thing. He never would have stayed in the midst of such profound heresy.

But the picture stuck in my head. I could see her standing up in that old church. Walking down the aisle. Out the door. And with that beautiful British accent saying, "I'm out."

Mrs. Hughes died a few years later. She'd hoped her pastors would be allowed to go back to the old church and bury her next to her husband. But that request was denied and she had to be buried elsewhere. The story is told that, at the request of the family, the late Mr. Hughes's casket was exhumed and buried next to his wife's.[1]

Nomads. Both of them. Even in death.

Because it's what we do. It's what we have to do when sin is in the camp.

Moses didn't stay. He couldn't stay. The calf was gone. The altar remained. But it was defiled. Like the people. Filled with sin. Big, serious, costly, breaking, corrupting sin.

So he took the Tent of Meeting. He went outside the camp.

Outside is where the unclean live. The lepers. Those who committed indecent acts of sin (Lev. 13:45–46; Num. 12:14–15). The destitute. The immoral. The condemned (Heb. 13:11–14).

He went out even beyond them. Out farther—to meet with the Lord. Because that's where the Lord was. Outside, not inside the camp. Not at the center. Not with the people.

Outside. Way outside.

Because He can't stay in. He won't stay in. Not when we allow sin—by choice—to reign at the center of our lives. Our church. Among our leaders.

The Lord said it and did it. Moses said it and did it. Mrs. Hughes said it and did it. Because there are times it has to be said. It has to be done.

I'm out.

QUESTIONS FOR REFLECTION

It is worth our time—our prayers—to reflect on the Lord's words here: "I will not go up in your midst." Have you experienced it? Making decisions you know were not godly and finding that He wasn't with you? Do you do that now?

It's hard when people we love choose to walk contrary to God—and expect us to do the same. Is it possible to love them, even stay with them, but not go with them? How do we love yet not condone? When is it right to say, "I'm out" and when is it not?

NOTE

1. Thaddeus Barnum, *Never Silent* (Colorado Springs: Eleison, 2008), 261, 359.

45

BREAK WITH THE PACK

Reflections on Exodus 33:7–11

*Now Moses used to take the tent and pitch it outside the
camp, a good distance from the camp, and he called it the
tent of meeting. And everyone who sought the LORD would go
out to the tent of meeting which was outside the camp.*

—EXODUS 33:7

I wonder how the news spread through the people.

The Lord was gone. Moses was gone. The worship of
God Most High, the God of Abraham, Isaac, and Jacob was
no longer in the center of the camp where His presence was
once strong with them. The cloud by day and fire by night
(see Num. 9:15–23).

Gone.

Moses had marched out by making a path through the
people. He strode through the camp. He broke past the line—
the great divide—which marked those who lived inside the
camp from those outside. But that line was meaningless now.
It used to separate the clean from the unclean. Those right
with God and those not.

But not now.

Not since the golden calf. Not since they put it in front
of the altar of the Lord and worshiped it, saying, "This is your

god, O Israel, who brought you up from the land of Egypt"
(Ex. 32:4).

Sin like no other.

Suddenly Moses was gone and he'd taken the Tent of
Meeting with him. Gone to seek the face of God. Gone, and
the gossip must have spread like wildfire through the camp.
Making people talk. Making them decide. Because some
stayed. Some didn't. Some broke with the pack and followed
Moses following the Lord.

It can actually be a difficult choice to make.

Years ago, I was appointed to a highly prestigious task
force. It was an honor to be asked. I couldn't believe the
names that sat around the table. People I'd heard about
from a distance and secretly admired.

At the first meeting, the chairman asked us to introduce
ourselves. We went around the room, and I remember feeling
quite embarrassed when it came to me. I had little to say. I
had done little in comparison to the rest of them. But people
were kind to me. They smiled, graciously, nodding with
approval. My tiny little self in the midst of giants.

But then the strangest thing happened. Out of the chairman's mouth came some opening remarks that shocked me.
I was completely taken aback. I thought maybe I misunder-
stood. So I spoke up and asked him to repeat it.

And he did. In such a lovely tone. With every intent to
bring blessing to his hearers. Wanting everyone to feel
comfortable and at ease.

"I realize," he said, "we're all Christian leaders and that
we're living in a day when there are general disagreements

about who Jesus is and what He came to do. But where we don't disagree is what's most important. All of us here believe that God is love and that He has called us to love Him and to love our neighbor." Then he smiled the biggest smile possible and said, "And that's what unites us! That's what will make us effective as a task force."

With that, the meeting got down to business. Everyone so pleasant and kind.

But this deeply troubled me. Did what happen just happen? Did he just set the Lord Jesus aside? Did he dismiss Him from the meeting? Did the chairman just say we disagree about Him, but we don't disagree about love? So we stick with love and boot Jesus out? Is that what I just heard?

I saw the image in my mind clear as day. Moses making a path through the people. But not Moses this time—the Lord Jesus Christ. He is no longer sitting at the table. He stands. He packs up His stuff. He looks around and begins to move, making a path through the people. He gets to the door, opens it, and He's gone.

And if He's gone, what am I still doing here?

But if I leave, what will these people think of me?

I can hear the argument in my head. I've heard it a thousand times: "Maybe the Lord is calling me to stay on the task force and be a witness to these Christian leaders."

But that's not it. Deep down, I wanted their approval. In many ways, I'm no different than the prominent Jewish leaders in Jesus' day who secretly believed in Him but refused to confess Him openly, publically, for one reason:

"They loved the approval of men rather than the approval of God" (John 12:43).

Was that me? Yes, it was me. I loved being at that table. I loved that these great people of reputation knew my name and would soon get to know me. This was an opportunity of a lifetime and could open big doors for the future. Yes, it could. Yes, it would.

The Lord was out. Why was I in?

I hesitated. I rationalized. But the words of Scripture kept thundering in my head: "Therefore Jesus also, that He might sanctify the people through His own blood, suffered outside the gate. So, let us go out to Him outside the camp, bearing His reproach. For here we do not have a lasting city, but we are seeking the city which is to come" (Heb. 13:12–14).

Jesus went outside the camp, just like Moses. But for Him, the path out was the path to His cross. It was the path of suffering and death. And the choice was there for me. It's there for all of us. Will we go with Him—out there?

It looks easy, sounds easy. It's not easy.

It's hard to break from the pack. It's hard not to long for the praise of others. It's harder, so much harder, when it's people we look up to—people with name and power and ability to impact our future. I wanted to stay. That's my sin. I wanted my name linked with theirs.

I struggled for the better part of a half hour. Then I packed up my stuff, stood up, and slipped quietly out the door.

QUESTIONS FOR REFLECTION

Approval is a big word for most of us. Sometimes without even knowing it, we make decisions based on what others decide. It is a hard question to ask: Is the approval of God in your life more important than the approval of others?

Making the decision to break from the crowd and go out to Him—to honor Him first, to bear His reproach—is often a costly choice. Can you make that choice? What hinders you? What helps you?

46

SHOW US YOUR GLORY

*Whenever Moses entered the tent, the pillar of cloud
would descend and stand at the entrance of the tent;
and the LORD would speak with Moses.*

—EXODUS 33:9

Politics. That's all that was left in the center of the camp.

Moses had bolted. He took the Tent of Meeting with him and went outside the camp. Outside where the forbidden dwelt—the unclean. He went out to meet with God because God had bolted too.

Away from His people. Away from the place the golden calf once stood. Away from politics. Because that's all that's left when the people of God meet together without Him.

And they do the unthinkable. Leaders jockeying for position. Leaders promising everything they have to please the majority of the people the majority of the time. Keep them happy. Keep them committed. Keep them coming back. Doing church without the Lord of the church anywhere near.

But that's not Moses.

He went where God went. Not to start a movement. Not to gather people, cast a vision, and then lead that vision for the people, with the people, by the people. His focus wasn't people. It wasn't politics.

It was God. It was the glory of God.

And it's what He did when they met together—He came down in glory. He descended in a pillar of cloud by day and a pillar of fire by night and filled the Tent of Meeting. Him! All Him! He was everything. He came to meet with Moses and Moses went to meet with Him, hear Him, talk to Him, and fall down in worship before Him.

Because without Him, everything falls apart. With Him, all things make sense.

And the people knew that. The ones who went out with Moses knew that. They didn't go out in rebellion to the old politics so they could start new politics. They went out because they sought the Lord. Just like Moses. And with the same prayer.

It's hard to keep this focus.

Not long ago, I had lunch with a great friend and senior pastor of a church in the Midwest. We had a good time together until I asked him how his church was going.

"I wasn't going to say anything," he lamented, "unless you asked. I hate to burden you with my problems."

"I want to know," I said. "I want to hear. What's going on?"

"My wife and I haven't slept well since this whole thing began," he started. "A number of our elders have been meeting together, on their own, without my knowledge, to start a campaign for change in the church. By the time I got wind of it, there was little I could do without causing a major rift with the leaders and within the church."

For the next hour and a half, my dear friend unraveled all the details of the story. It broke my heart to see the breaking of his heart.

"It sounds like politics to me," I groaned.

"What do you mean by that?" he said, surprised.

"I mean this isn't you. It's never been you. It's what I love about you, your passion for the Lord. You never give up. You never tire. You pursue Him in prayer. You pursue Him in service. When I've been to your church, I see that same passion in the heart of the people. Your face, their faces, turned to His."

"That's what gets me up every morning," he agreed.

"But all that changes," I said, "when our faces turn inward. We take our eyes—our hearts—off Jesus Christ and put them on this issue or that issue. Without even blinking, we take sides. Divisions break out. People get hurt. Meetings take place and, though we pray, we're all lost in the big issue of the moment."

"I tell you," he stated firmly, "it sucks the life right out of me."

"Yeah, well, I call it church politics. Because that's what happens when any issues in the church take center stage."

"And become bigger than Him," he added.

"Yeah, so it's a choice. Do we turn our faces to Him? Do we put Him in the center of our issues, our problems, our concerns, our relationships? Do we seek Him together as leaders—as a church family—until He speaks into our story?"

"Or do we turn on each other," he said painfully, "which is exactly what's happening to us right now. I know it's happening to me. Over the last five or six weeks it's been all-consuming. It's all I've been thinking about."

Caught up in the mess.

It's hard to keep focus. Really hard.

"You know," I recalled, "you're the one who taught me this. 'Keep your focus on Jesus, Barnum!' you always say. And you do it so well. You turn your face to His and you help the rest of us do the same. I thank God for you, dear friend. You are a consummate pastor—not a politician. This needs to end. This is not you."

He sat back in his chair and took a deep breath. He slowly nodded his head and then smiled at me.

"OK, I'll do it," he whispered.

Just like Moses.

He decided then and there to get his eyes off the big, bad issue at church and do what he knew to do—seek the Lord. He'd set his face to seek the face of God. He'd have to trust that there'd be people in the church who would do the same. They'd go with him, though some wouldn't. But for most of them, he knew it was there—deep within them—that relentless passion that always, always, puts the lordship of Jesus Christ at the very center of the church, the center of our issues, and the center of our lives.

That relentless pursuit for Him to come down. For the Holy Spirit to fill the church as He once filled the Tent of Meeting.

And that relentless prayer.

Show us Your glory.

QUESTIONS FOR REFLECTION

We need politics in society. But in the church, it's meant to be different. The Lord takes center stage, not us, and not our issues. What happens to you when your eyes get off Him and your issues become all-consuming?

Sometimes, especially with chronic issues, this choice is daily. Even hourly. Sometimes we need others around us to help us with it. Do you have this discipline in your life— to choose to seek Him? To ask Him to fill you—and fill your church—with His Spirit? To seek His glory?

47

REVIVALS

Reflections on Exodus 33:9–11

Thus the LORD used to speak to Moses face to face,
just as a man speaks to his friend.

—EXODUS 33:11

He stays away.

He used to have reasons why. All perfectly sound. Meticulously defensible. It just that he's forgotten most of them.

Too many years have passed. Now decades. He rarely thinks about it. Once, maybe twice a year, an old memory comes to mind. A person from the past calls. He hears an odd turn of phrase. But like a nagging mosquito, he swats the air, barely giving it the time of day.

He made choices then. He's lived so long in those choices that the possibility of going back to the way things were never crosses his mind.

Every few years he goes home. He's there but not there. He stays a day. Maybe two or three.

It's all part of my friend's story. Something happened a long time ago. Something no one knows but him. Early on, his family did everything they could to figure it out. To apologize. To help his soul heal from whatever it was. But his heart turned away and never turned back. Eventually, they stopped trying. Wanting to respect his decision. Feeling guilty they were powerless to do anything about it.

Secrets buried deep in his soul. Hurts that never see the light of day.

He does life well. Work, family, church, friends. So well, in fact, that no one around him, even those who know him best, have any idea of his past. Or that there are wounds scarred on his heart. Or that he belongs to a family far away who grieves in pain without him. They love him. Pray for him. Miss him.

Wanting him home, but he stays away.

His family never forgets. Never stops praying. Never stops believing that the day will come and he will be home. Really home. His heart home. That whatever this thing is, the terrible monster of the past, the unforgiveable crime that has so deeply cut his soul will be — can be — healed. In Jesus Christ. By Jesus Christ.

They do the only thing they know to do. They go to Him. They wait for Him.

It's exactly what Moses did. In a day when sin had ripped through and divided the people of God, Moses did the only thing he knew to do.

He went out to Him. Outside the camp.

He went out and set up the Tent of Meeting and waited on the Lord. Waited until He came down in the glory of the pillar of cloud. And he didn't wait alone. There were people with the same heart. Standing at a distance. Waiting with him.

It's how revivals happen.

The people of God break from the crowd. Break from the sin in the world. Break from the sin in the church. With one passion. One fire in their bellies.

"Oh, that You would rend the heavens and come down, that the mountains might quake at Your presence" (Isa. 64:1).

Revivals are never worked up. They don't require great orators, charismatic leaders, or exceptional visionaries able to motivate and inspire people to follow. They require only one thing. A heart passionately waiting for the Lord.

Revivals are an act of God come down. And when He comes, there are people waiting. Praying. Expecting. And the moment He comes, they do what the saints have always done. They fall down before Him and worship Him.

And then He does what He's always done. He speaks to them. With mercy, compassion, and kindness. With intimacy that leaps beyond imagining.

It's the story of Pentecost.

The disciples were there, praying, waiting, expecting. And the Holy Spirit came down in power, just as the Lord Jesus had promised. And when He came, Peter stood up, opened his mouth, and the Lord spoke to His people through him.

And they worshiped the Lord. The people who were there saw and heard and experienced the real, true descent of the pillar of cloud. And miracle of all miracles, those looking on confessed their sins, repented, and received the forgiveness found in Jesus' name.

Those deep secrets. Those terrible monsters of the past. Those unforgiveable crimes that wound the soul to its very core and then bitterly poison the course of our lives.

Washed away. All of it. In Jesus Christ. By Jesus Christ.

We need revivals. The saints have known this down through the centuries. It's the only way we can do the work He's called us to do. To reach the world with the power of this saving gospel and to extend our hearts to help the poor, needy, lonely, and afflicted. To reconcile those who don't know. To reconcile those who stay away.

Like my friend. He stays away.

So his family does the only thing they know to do. They go to Him. They wait for Him. Praying. Expecting. Believing, always believing a day will come when he'll come home. Really home.

His heart home.

QUESTIONS FOR REFLECTION

There's a way to be Christian—live Christian—and have secrets, wounds, and hurts rooted deep inside us that are untouched by the Lord. Is that you? Are they still there, defining you?

There is an intimacy that comes with revivals. The Lord meets with us and we know it. He does a work inside us—a cleansing work, a healing work, an empowering work—and we are changed. Do you know this? Believe this? Want this? Long for this? If not, why not?

48

WE MUST GO

Reflections on Hebrews 13:12–14

So, let us go out to Him outside the camp, bearing His reproach. For here we do not have a lasting city, but we are seeking the city which is to come.

—HEBREWS 13:13–14

I wish I lived in times, in places, of revival. I wish I could experience those days when the Lord visits His church in power and everything comes alive. Where "the blind receive sight and the lame walk, the lepers are cleansed and the deaf hear, the dead are raised up, and the poor have the gospel preached to them" (Matt. 11:5).

And the Lord comes down.

Like He did in the days of Moses who went outside the camp. Breaking from the crowd. Breaking from the sin of their golden calf to seek the face of God. And the glory of God came down and the Lord visited His people.

Like He did in the days when He sent His Son to be with us and the people came from everywhere to behold His glory. To see His miracles. To touch His garment and feel the rush of eternal life coursing through every fiber of their beings.

Like He did in the days of old when the church was dead, formal, cold, devoid of the Holy Spirit, and full of corruption, greed, and evil practices. And those who believed begged Him to come down and fill His church again with Pentecost fire.

History records those moments when He did. I love reading about them. I dream of being inside them — always. As if, somehow, I could slip into the fantastical world of Narnia and behold Aslan as he brings everything to life.

If this is what it means to follow Jesus Christ, sign me up. I'm in. But don't sign me up for the other, please.

A man my age calls me and asks me for help. He's going through tough days.

I tell him I will because it's the right thing to do. To be honest, I don't want to. Not this time. Of course, I don't tell him that. I can't. Because I know what he's asking of me. I know what it will cost me.

He's hurting. Deeply. There's anguish in his soul. He's done his best to handle it, but he's come to the end of his ability and he needs someone to come alongside and help.

"Will you go with me?"

I've been here before — so many times. I know this story. And every time I come here I remember the first bishop I served under. He made me come here. He'd call me up and tell me a story of someone in need. In suffering. In pain. And that I was to go and be with them. In their heartache and grief. And not just for a moment.

"Will you go with me?"

Not a flyby. Zoom in. Put on a sad face. Stay a few minutes. Lay hands on the sick. Pray with eloquence and power in Jesus' name.

And zoom out.

He taught me to stay there—in their suffering. Stay and not leave. Go with them—no matter how long it takes. No matter how much it costs. See the journey through to the end. Always.

"Will you go with me?"

And why, I'd ask. "Because that's the story. That's the whole story," he'd answer. And on he'd go, telling me this is exactly what Jesus Christ meant when He commanded us to follow Him. "This is the road we go because this is the road He took. Never forget that. And never say you won't go."

So I went. At first because he told me to. And then because I knew it was the right thing to do. Never say no even though, most times, I wanted to say different.

I wanted to say no.

Sign me up for the other. Give me those special days of revival when Aslan is in town and the sick are always healed. The suffering suffer no more. Our prayers are always answered. And I don't have to take these journeys. These long, costly journeys.

For many years, I saw two completely different roads. The road of revival Moses took outside the camp that led to seeing the power and glory of God. And the dreaded other. The road the suffering take in the days when it feels like our Lord is gone and we are left alone.

I didn't understand it yet. I didn't understand that Jesus Christ is there—on both roads. That because of Him, the road of suffering and the road of revival are one and the same. He proved that when He was here. There were days He healed all who came to Him. And then there was the day He broke from the crowd, forged a path out to Calvary's hill, turned to His disciples, like He does to all of us, and told them to follow Him.

"Will you go with Me?"

Two roads become one.

He tells us the road of suffering is the only way to His glory. And if we wish to go with Him, certain things are required. We must deny ourselves, take up our cross, and follow Him (Mark 8:34). I always find myself fighting this.

"Will you go with Me?"

But I don't want to go. Not on that road. Give me the road of revival. Don't give me the road of suffering. I want one, not the other.

"But that's the story," my bishop would say. "That's the whole story."

We must go to Him. Outside the camp. Bearing His reproach.

"This is the road we go," my bishop taught me, "because this is the road He took. Never forget that. And never say you won't go."

No flybys. Stay. Always stay. See the journey to the end. And why?

Because that's where Jesus is. It's where He always is. When the glory comes down, He is there. When the suffering comes, He is there. And where He is, everything comes alive.

"Will you go with Me?"

QUESTIONS FOR REFLECTION

Do you know what it's like to see Jesus in the midst of suffering—yours or someone else's? To feel His presence, to know His power, to hear His words of comfort though the suffering continues?

Will you go with Him, regardless of what it will cost you? Regardless of which road it is? And will you stay till you see the journey to the end?

PART 7

ACCESS IN JESUS

49
"YES!" ALWAYS

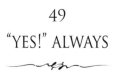

Reflections on John 14:1–6

*Jesus said to him, "I am the way, and the truth, and the life;
no one comes to the Father but through Me."*

—JOHN 14:6

"No!" he thundered, pounding his fist on the table, his face turning beet red. He immediately stood, ready to speak his mind.

We'd pushed him too far.

Erilynne and I were leading a retreat for the leaders of a church. We were dealing with one of the most important questions church elders can ask: "Lord, where can we serve, what can we do as a church family, to meet the needs of our community in Your name?"

May sound simple, but this question touches everything. It means we believe in Jesus Christ as the Bible reveals Him. We believe He is Lord of His church, that He has a plan for His church, and that it's His desire to guide us into that plan as He so chooses.

It means we believe it's His desired will to speak to us as we meet in prayer, worship, fellowship, and study of His

Word. It means we submit to His lordship in our lives as we seek Him, hear Him, and choose to obey Him. It means we have to start with this question: Is Jesus Christ who He said He is?

May sound simple.

With one heart, one voice, these church leaders rejoiced to say, "Yes, Jesus is who He said He is in the Bible. He's our Savior, Lord, and Lord of this church."

The man sitting across from us had been as happy as he could be. He'd spoken up on several occasions and made His love for Jesus Christ known. But his mood quickly changed when we turned our attention to John 14:6 and said, "Jesus Christ is the Way, that's what He taught. He's the only way to the Father. No one comes to the Father but through Him. That means He's not just the only way for us, He's the only way for everybody, everywhere."

The man became quiet, simmering.

Minutes later, he exploded, fist on the table. At first, he argued for the millions of people in different religions who truly love God and don't accept the belief that Jesus is Savior and Lord. Then he argued for the millions of people who are basically, in their heart, good people and who love God but don't know—or even reject—Jesus.

"He's the way for me," he protested. "He's Lord of my life and I know He's Lord of this church. That's my belief. But I don't push Him onto others. And I don't judge people who don't believe in Him like I do. And that's what you're doing!"

And then he thundered again, pointing his finger at us, "No!"

It's happened before. If we say emphatically, as Jesus said, "No one comes to the Father but through [Him]," we're often labeled "exclusive," "arrogant," "rigid," and "intolerant." We're told it's wrong to think that Jesus Christ, and Christianity in general, is God's only way of saving the human race. The only entrance card into heaven.

I grew up in a Christian denomination that, in recent years, finally rejected the Bible's view that salvation is found only in Jesus Christ. In a meeting of their top leaders and officials, they refused to support a resolution upholding Acts 4:12: "And there is salvation in no one else; for there is no other name under heaven that has been given among men by which we must be saved."

Later, the head of the denomination told *Time* magazine, "To think that God could not act in other ways is, I think, to put God in an awfully small box."[1]

To be honest, I understand this reaction. I am not so unlike them or the man who screamed, "No!"

It's a word I've used a lot in my life. Call me arrogant, and I agree because I've spent a lot of my life saying no to God.

"No!" when the culture tells me it's right and He's says it's wrong. "No!" when I think I have the right to believe whatever I want to believe. "No!" when my prayers for those I love who are suffering aren't answered the way I want and I think, if I were Him, I would have done different. Better. "No!" when He uncovers my sin and tells me to stop. "No!" when He shows me what to do and I don't want to do it. "No! No! No!"

It's called rebellion. Pride. Sin. It was there, inside me, to say no to my parents when I was a toddler and no to God when I became an adult. And sometimes I want to do exactly what this man did. Stand up. Pound my fist on the table. Turn bright red in the face. And speak my mind.

He sat back down and told us his story.

For him, only one thing mattered. He needed to know that his parents were in heaven. He loved them so much. When they died, his entire world fell apart. He ran into the arms of Jesus for comfort. He leaned on his church family for help and support. Even now, years later, he missed his parents so much.

"They were good people," he told us. "They believed in God their way. I told them about Jesus but they didn't want to hear. And I can't believe, no, I *won't* believe that they're not in heaven. God wouldn't do that. Not the God I love."

The room fell silent. A few people got up and came around him to comfort him and pray for him. No one had expected this. Or the rush of emotions. Or the stark realization of the grief he carried in his heart.

May sound simple. But it's not.

Submitting to the lordship of Jesus Christ means saying "Yes!" to Him. "Yes!" He is who He said He is. "Yes!" the Bible is the Word of the Lord to us, even when we don't know how to wrestle with life's hardest questions . . . or the sufferings of this man's heart. "Yes!" in our confusions. "Yes!" in our rebellion. "Yes!" when nothing makes sense. "Yes!" to trust Him with all our hearts, our hurts, and our lives.

Because He's God.

So we say yes in humility. In reverence. Even when everything inside us wants to say no.

"Yes!" always.

QUESTIONS FOR REFLECTION

Do you know the places inside you today that are screaming no to God? Are you going to hold onto them, or are you willing to let Him help you with them?

Some of these questions—like, "What happens to the billions who are not Christians?"—block people from coming to Christ. There comes a time when we must surrender these questions to God and come as He has said. Are you able to surrender? Are you willing to come?

NOTE

1. Thaddeus Barnum, *Never Silent* (Colorado Springs, Eleison, 2008), 251.

50

CRAZED REBELLION

Reflections on Leviticus 16

*Tell your brother Aaron that he shall not enter at any
time into the holy place inside the veil, before the mercy
seat which is on the ark, or he will die; for I will
appear in the cloud over the mercy seat.*

—LEVITICUS 16:2

I was twelve. Summer had come and my parents had decided to kick me out of the nest for the month of July. First time, and it scared me. It scared me so much that I became defiant. I did everything I could to try and get out of it. I tried reason. I tried emotion. I tried distancing myself and withdrawing. I tried a thousand different things to send the message loud and clear.

I wasn't going.

I refused, and they couldn't make me.

But they did. They weathered through my tantrums, packed me up and off I went, panic-stricken with swollen eyes from crying and not sleeping. I kept asking why they were doing this to me and they kept answering that it was for the best. For my benefit. That one day I'd understand.

I wanted to hate them for this. But that's the crazy thing. I didn't want to leave them because I loved them. And I loved our home, my brother, my sister, our dog, our lazy summers, and our long weekends. I was safe there. It's all I knew. It's all I wanted to know. And I knew they loved me. I knew they wanted the best for me. I trusted that. I always trusted that.

It's why I said yes when they asked me to do what I wanted to do. It's why I said yes when they asked me to do what I didn't want to do.

But this? This was different. This stirred in me a rebellion that put me at war with myself. Hating the ones I loved. Afraid of a world without them. Afraid something terrible would happen to them and I'd never see them again, never see home. Or something would happen to me, and then what?

And I felt it. Deep inside me.

A crazed rebellion.

On first hearing, it sounds odd. Even wrong. I taught a Bible study once and a person laughed out loud saying, "I thank God your God isn't my God!"

"Why?" I asked back.

"Because I can go to Him anytime I want!"

As if His door is always open. As if we're welcome at any time. Having no idea what it cost to open that door. No idea that for the longest time that door was closed. Shut tight. And we didn't have access at any time to run in and out of His presence, pray what we want to pray, do what we want to do.

Shut tight.

That's how it all started, beginning the day we were kicked out of Eden. The Lord, the God who made heaven and earth, slammed the door so loud that it echoed down through the centuries with a clear and unmistakable message.

No access. Not on your terms.

Access only on My terms.

At first, He doesn't tell us why. It was enough that this was His decision and He expected us to do what He said because He's our Father and our God. Because He knows what's best for us. Because He loves us with an everlasting love.

The door closed. Shut tight. We can't go in and out when we want. The only way in is to do it His way. And His way isn't easy. It's hard. It's filled with deep, personal loss and costly sacrifice. For us. For Him.

And so He told Moses to erect a tent, a tabernacle, where He would come and meet with His people. His throne room, called the Holy of Holies, had a way in and that way was shut. The closed door was actually a huge, thick veil. The Lord told Moses to tell his brother Aaron, the high priest, one thing: He can't come in when he wants, at any time. No one can.

At the command of God, the high priest was the only one allowed in. As our representative. Once a year. Not on his terms. God's terms.

Not his way, God's way.

I sat at an old man's bedside in the hospital room. He knew he was about to die and reassured me he was "at peace with his Maker." But his eyes were wild, darting. He was angry with me. "Yes, I believe I'm going to heaven," he argued, picking up an old conversation we'd had a few years before. "And yes, I'm going to see my loved ones again. Yes, I believe in God, but no, I'm not doing the Jesus thing. Do you understand me?"

I told him I did.

I told him the story of when I was twelve and how I hated my parents, whom I so desperately loved, because they were making me do what I didn't want to do. I was scared to leave home. Scared of what might happen to me. To them.

"They told me to trust them," I said. "That I'd understand later in life. And they were right. Looking back all these years later, I know they loved me enough to do what was right for me, what was best. They knew it was time for me to grow up—and I didn't want to. But me?" I smiled, remembering. "Defiant to the core. I felt it. Deep inside me. I wasn't going. I refused. I knew better than they did."

He turned away. I saw his hand next to me ball up into a tight fist as if, maybe, he understood my defiance and his were one and the same.

And I felt it again. Like I have so many times in my life. A crazed rebellion.

QUESTIONS FOR REFLECTION

Jesus said in Matthew 11:29, "Take My yoke upon you and learn from Me." A young bull doesn't want to be hitched to an older one. Do that and we lose our freedom. But this is where life in Jesus begins. Are you willing to be yoked to Him? To do things His way, not yours?

Do you know what access to God means? What it cost? What great lengths He's gone to for us to be able to come before Him? Does it stir inside you a deeper love for Him?

51

A THOUSAND WALLS

Reflections on Exodus 26:31–35

You shall make a veil of blue and purple and scarlet material and fine twisted linen; it shall be made with cherubim, the work of a skillful workman.

—Exodus 26:31

I put down the phone and groaned.

I'd hurt my friend. My good, dear, old, and trusted friend. I could hear it in his voice. He was distant and unengaged. I wanted to chat like we always do, natural and easy, where time flies by without even knowing it. But not today. He couldn't get through the conversation fast enough.

Something was wrong, terribly wrong.

My mind raced back to our last meeting. We'd had a difficult conversation that day. There were four of us, our wives included, and we'd had tough issues to face and resolve. Although there were moments of sharp disagreement, there was a deep sense of trust between us that gave us the freedom to talk through these issues. And we ended that time well— at least, I thought we did. We all seemed to be at peace with each other.

But something must have happened. Something I said. Something I did. I immediately replayed the meeting in my mind, over and over. What did I do? What did I say? And it came back to me. Words that were too strong.

A tongue too loose.

And now this wall stood between us, separating us. A wall that could be felt. Like I could reach out my hand and touch it.

I know that wall well. I've put it up a thousand times. I learned how to early on. When someone hurt me, just step back. When I didn't like someone, when I didn't trust them, just step back. Even those I deeply love, will always love, the moment something didn't go my way, just step back and build the wall.

Build it physically and stay away. Build it emotionally and withdraw.

Send the message loud and clear or send it disguised with a smile and shallow conversation, it doesn't matter. Just send it.

Something is wrong, terribly wrong.

God does walls too. He had to. He had no choice. We hurt Him. We betrayed Him. We committed a crime against Him that stabbed at the very heart of our relationship with Him. Rending us apart. Causing massive separation between us.

We did this. Forcing Him to turn away. Forcing Him to hide His face: "But your iniquities have made a separation between you and your God, and your sins have hidden His face from you so that He does not hear" (Isa. 59:2).

And so He made it real.

He commanded Moses to set up a tabernacle, a tent where He'd come down and dwell in the midst of His people. He commanded a room be set apart, the Holy of Holies, where He would sit "enthroned above the cherubim" (Ps. 80:1; 99:1).

But there'd be a wall, a thick veil, between us.

Separating us. Forcing us to face the story, the real story—something is wrong, terribly wrong. Sin had come into the world. Sin, evil, and death. And not just into the world, into us. Reigning in us. And by the decree of almighty God, that veil would not come down until the problem between us was resolved.

The problem. The sin. The horror of our crimes, our betrayal.

And so we did what we always do. We ran away, set up our own tabernacles of worship, and created gods of our own. Gods who look like us. Think like us. And who don't put up veils between us, blocking our access so we can run to them anytime we want. Worship them. Pray to them. Gods who don't make us face the one and only God who, by His command, demands we confront the separation between us.

And then let Him do what only He can do. Tear down the wall, the veil, once and forever, "from top to bottom" (Matt. 27:51).

I called my friend a few days later and asked if we could meet.

We met at a local diner. Cordial, but not the same. I did my best in the opening minutes to see if the wall was really there. It was. Big, thick, course to the touch. And I knew I had to confront it straight on.

"I'm sorry I hurt you."

I've been here before. So many times. And it never gets easier because what's easier is to avoid it altogether. We hurt people or people hurt us and we put up a wall—a thousand walls—because we don't want to deal with it. We choose to move on. We pray it'll go away on its own or that one day the pain inside us won't hurt so much. And the wall stands—for a month, a year, a lifetime.

Never saying sorry.

Sorry for the wrong we've done. Sorry for the wall standing between us. Sorry that the love we've shared has been stolen from us. Ripped from our hearts.

"I'm sorry I hurt you."

I had to learn to do this. As a Christian. To take first steps. To not talk around the wall or avoid it like the elephant in the room. But to face it head-on. And to pray the Lord, in His kindness, steps in. That He does what we can't do ourselves—heal our broken hearts. Make the walls come crashing down. Allowing us to say what we need to say: "I forgive you in Jesus' name."

But not today.

The wounds were still fresh. The pain too deep. This would take time. But more than time, it would take choice. Choice to see it through to the end. Or choice to walk out our days with the wall still between us.

And I saw it in his eyes. Oh, thank God I saw it.

He wanted the wall to come down as much as I did.

QUESTIONS FOR REFLECTION

Can you count the walls in your life? Between you and the Lord? You and those closest to you? Walls even inside you—places blocked off that you refuse to confront?

As He tears down the wall between us and Him, we learn to do the same with others and ourselves. Just as He did it, we do it. Are you willing? Will you try it this week? Will you ask Him to help you with one wall, even just one?

52

WAY BEYOND SORRY

Reflections on Leviticus 17:11 and Hebrews 9:22

Without shedding of blood there is no forgiveness.
—HEBREWS 9:22

He was cold and ruthless.

It's like he got in his eighteen-wheel Mack truck, revved the engines, and tore off. Not caring that his friends, his closest friends—even his wife—were standing in the middle of the road.

And he drove it hard. Drove it fast. Right over them. No looking back. All the while, telling himself he's right. It's not his fault. He's able to list the reasons why he did what he did—the perfect, ironclad defense. While those he loves lay on the side of the road bleeding.

That's Ron. He sinned, sinned big. After nineteen years of marriage, he ran into the arms of another woman. Not once, but twice. He blamed it on a "loveless marriage" and knew he needed "a way out."

There are those who just keep driving. Never looking in the rearview mirror. Never counting the bodies lying on the side of the road. Never caring because caring requires a heart that can still feel—feel the guilt, feel the shame, feel the hurt they've caused. But their heart is cold—so they drive. Drive hard.

While others look back. They stare in the rearview mirror. They can see the pain they've caused those they love. They know their sin, their wrong. They know they have to stop, pull over, and do something about it.

Ron had to stop. He called a friend. He told him what he'd done. His friend told the story to his wife. His wife then called Ron and encouraged him to tell Ron's wife, Deborah, and if he didn't, she said she would.

Ron had to get out of his big, bad truck and go to the crime scene. He had to face a world of devastation and unspeakable pain that he, in his stupid, selfish, lust-driven sin had caused. How does he say sorry to the other woman he wrongfully used for his own pleasure? How does he face his wife of nineteen years?

Ron described what happened when he told his wife:

Then I went home and confessed to Deborah. My spin: Her disinterest had driven me into the arms of another woman, one who wanted me just the way I am—money and all.

"What!" she screamed, flying into a rage. "Nineteen years! Nineteen years! What were you thinking? How could you do this?"

Shoes, vases, and figurines flew through the air, some a direct hit. When nothing else presented itself as a weapon, Deborah pounded me with her bare fists until her arms wore out and hung limp at her sides.

The night spun by in a whirl of sleepless anger. The next morning we phoned our pastor.[1]

He'd committed the act weeks before. He'd run that big, bad truck over his wife the second he decided to take the other woman into his arms and not look back.

But now he got to see the replay in real time. He got to see his wife's eyes as the words came out of his mouth and the news broke over her soul. Her eyes, as the gunshot of his sin came barreling at her at full force, crushing her heart. Smashing nineteen years of trust into smithereens.

The word *sorry* simply didn't work. He'd gone way beyond sorry.

The call to the pastor was the right thing to do. Pastors know—or at least, they should know—what to do at times like these. Actually, every Christian should know.

In the Old Testament, people would go to the sanctuary with a live offering (a goat or lamb) and stand before the priest. They'd place "one hand on the head of the animal, make confession of the sin, and then with the other hand, slay the animal. A priest would catch the blood in a basin. . . . In the Old Testament, forgiveness of sin was granted whenever confession was made (for example, Ps. 32:5); the sacrifice symbolically completed the process, showing that forgiveness was based on the shedding of blood. The confession without the ritual was incomplete, but the ritual without confession was worthless."[2]

It was never enough just to say sorry.

Sin costs. It always costs. If we want to know forgiveness—real, God-given forgiveness—then we do it His way. And His way requires an offering for sin. A sacrifice. It requires that we face the horror and devastation of our sin.

In the eyes of a little lamb.

So we make our confession. But we never leave it there. We have to go through the Lord's ritual. Our hand on the head of the lamb. Our sin transferred. The death of the lamb for us because of what we did. We have to see it, experience it, and know that our sin costs, costs deeply—as we watch the little lamb die.

This is God's way. There must be the shedding of blood in order to receive the Father's gift of the forgiveness of our sin (Heb. 9:22). And what He taught us in the Old Testament, He fulfilled in the New. And because of it, we know what to do today.

We know where to go to make our confession. Though the offering has already been made once and for all, we still have to walk through the ritual. We still have to face the horror and devastation of our sin.

In the eyes of the Lamb of God.

Ron and Deborah went to their pastor. They went to counseling. They made a commitment to rewrite the future of their marriage.

But Deborah knew more, so much more.

She grabbed Ron's hand and led him to the local rescue mission in Fort Worth, Texas. She wanted him to see the homeless and addicted, the poor and needy, the beaten and

broken. Because she knew Jesus was there. And she knew
the only way to get her husband back, for their marriage to
be healed and forgiven, was for Ron to meet Jesus Christ.

It didn't seem possible. How could anyone meet Jesus
by spending week after week coming alongside the homeless and poor?

But Deborah knew, yes she knew. And that's exactly
what happened.

QUESTIONS FOR REFLECTION

The first step to real identity in Jesus is confession.
Always confession. We face the story about ourselves—
our sin, our cold, hard hearts. Are you still driving hard and
not looking back?

For many, the idea that forgiveness requires cost—
requires blood—is foreign. Absurd. Unthinkable. But it's
God's way. Always has been, from the days of Abel and
Cain. Have you thought deeply on Hebrews 9:22? Do you
know the cost to forgive—and to be forgiven?

NOTES

1. Ron Hall and Denver Moore, *Same Kind of Different as Me: A Modern-Day Slave, an International Art Dealer, and the Unlikely Woman Who Bound Them Together* (Nashville: Thomas Nelson, 2006), 68.

2. Allen P. Ross, *Recalling the Hope of Glory: Biblical Worship from the Garden to the New Creation* (Grand Rapids, Mich.: Kregel, 2006), 198–199.

53

WE MUST WAIT

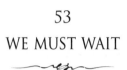

Reflections on Leviticus 17:11

*For the life of the flesh is in the blood, and I have given
it to you on the altar to make atonement for your souls;
for it is the blood by reason of the life that makes atonement.*

—LEVITICUS 17:11

I admire my friend so much.

He's not the guy driving the eighteen-wheel, Mack truck, hard and fast, running over people, leaving a trail of hurt and broken people in his wake.

He's the guy who keeps getting hit.

And he's the guy who knows exactly what to do. He does it over and over again. He goes to Jesus. He confesses *his* sin, even though he's the one being sinned against. But he knows what the Lord requires of him. He knows his own anger, the outbursts of his tongue, and the bitterness of his soul.

He goes to Jesus. He prays with his wife. He prays with a few close brothers and sisters in Christ. And we pray over him. We pray for protection. We pray for healing and mercy. But more than anything, we pray the blood of our Lord Jesus Christ over him, asking the Lord to grant His forgiveness to bless our dear friend.

He knows he needs it. Desperately needs it. Because he doesn't want to spend the rest of his life constantly reacting to the Mack-man driving that eighteen-wheeler over his crushed soul.

Because that Mack-man was his boss. And that Mack-man was a Christian leader, a man of great reputation and fame in his community.

Eventually, my friend found other employment and the Lord gave blessings to his work and family. But six months after, eighteen months after, three years after, he'd still be talking about the Mack-man—the pain he caused, the pain he continues to cause others.

He still goes to Jesus.

"It's like I finally get to that place," he told me, "where I've given it to Jesus. I've confessed my own anger and hatred for the man. For this short window of time, I get a taste of the Lord's forgiveness. It feels like it's over, like I can close that chapter in my life and move on with my eyes finally off him and on to the Lord Jesus. But then it comes back in full force. Just the mention of his name, or some news of someone else he's hurt, and my insides tighten into a knot. Before I know it, I can't stop thinking about him, talking about him, and it's like the anger and bitterness is worse than before."

So he goes to Jesus.

"I keep giving it to Him, over and over" he tells me. "Then, before I know it, I take it right back."

He's tired. He wants it to be over. But he doesn't know what else to do.

We go back. Back to the Old Testament. Back to where the Lord taught us, in great detail and with great precision, how to receive the forgiveness of our sins.

It starts with confession. We have to have the courage to speak it out loud. All of it. Not in self-defense, but on our knees in humility before the Lord.

In those days, our hands would rest on the head of the sacrifice so that our sins would be transferred to the animal. Without the shedding of blood, the Bible teaches everywhere, there is no forgiveness of sin (Heb. 9:22). For this reason, the animal, now bearing our sins, dies. Dies for us, as us. But there's more. The ritual is not done.

We must wait.

This is hard for some of us. We want to run to Jesus—our Lamb of God, our holy, once-and-for-all sacrifice. Repent and confess our sin. Receive His forgiveness and that's that. Done. Over. What else is needed?

We must wait.

The priest has work to do. This is especially seen on the Day of Atonement when the high priest was given special access through the veil, into the very presence of God, in the Holy of Holies. He would carry in the blood. And there the high priest would pray for the people. This was his job. As he sprinkled the blood on the mercy seat, he would intercede before God on their behalf.

And it's still His job.

To this day, our great High Priest, the Lord Jesus Christ, goes before His Father to "make intercession" for us. That's what He does (see Rom. 8:34; Heb. 7:25; Rev. 5:8; 8:4).[1]

We must wait.

"When he goes in to make atonement in the holy place, no one shall be in the tent of meeting until he comes out" (Lev. 16:17).

Wait until He comes out.

If we don't wait, we'll keep giving it to Him and taking it back. Giving it to Him and taking it back. We must wait, wait until He comes out, wait until He comes with the gift in His hand—the best gift of all—and gives it to us, so that we open our hands and receive it. The forgiveness of our sin. And not just sin in general. This sin—in particular.

My friend—I admire him so much.

He taught me how to wait. He did it by showing me how hard it was. Like him, I'm massively impatient. I'm part of the fast-food generation so, naturally, I want to go to Jesus, confess my sin, and get His blessing. Story over. But that's not the way it works. Never has. Never will.

He did it. I watched him. He waited.

One day he called me and said what I'd hoped to hear. It was over. Really, really over. The scars were still there. He expected relapses from time to time. But the pain, anger, and bitterness were safe in the hands of Jesus.

"I wish I could explain it to you," he said to me. "It was like this gift came into my heart and made me whole again. I could now, in earnest, pray for this man's soul—and pray with a new freedom. He no longer has power over me, does that make sense? I feel like I can now go to those he's tormented and give them hope in Jesus—real hope."

The gift was his and, he told me, it was worth the wait.

QUESTIONS FOR REFLECTION

Many of us live in the endless cycle of giving it and taking it back. We don't know about the waiting part—and the expecting part. Is there something in you that has hope, real hope, that the pain you carry will one day be safely given to Jesus and never given back?

Praying for those who've hurt us—loving our enemies—doesn't come naturally to the human heart. It's a kingdom act. It comes only when the Lord has done a work inside us. And when He does, we find freedom to pray like never before. Is this something you know about? Is it something you're willing to ask the Lord for?

NOTE

1. When the high priest entered the Holy of Holies, the incense from the golden altar would fill the room. This incense, the Bible teaches, is a picture of the "prayers of the saints" (Rev. 5:8; 8:4).

54

BALLOONS

Reflections on Leviticus 16:20–22

The goat shall bear on itself all their iniquities to a solitary land.

—LEVITICUS 16:22

He sits in church. Staring at the preacher in the pulpit.

It all comes back. The accusations and gossip. Angry words said to his face. Said behind his back then told to him, or told to his wife or to his friends. It happened sixteen years ago. But it feels like it happened three weeks ago.

"You see that man?" a fellow Christian whispered to a new family joining the church. "He used to be a preacher. Got caught in a sex scandal that made the papers and everything. Said it was an underage teen girl."

It wasn't. But it doesn't matter. It's what people believe. And every couple of years, the whispers in the church turn to a loud thunderous roar.

"Keep your young daughters away from him."

"Sexual offender . . ."

"People like that never change . . ."

He hates what it does to his wife. His family. His close friends. No matter what he does, where he goes, it's like he wears a big bull's-eye on his chest. And when he least expects it, hunting season opens all over again.

Over the years, he's fought the urge to stand up, tell people what really happened, so at least when they accuse him they get the story straight. But that doesn't matter either. The fact is, he did mess up. He exercised poor judgment. He crossed boundaries he knew not to cross. When he was caught, disciplined, tossed out of the pulpit, and labeled a sex offender, he knew the perception would never change. And he knew, at least in part, it was true. He was a sex offender. He'd never be entrusted with the pulpit again. Ever. He'd never get the bull's-eye off his back.

A year and a half after his crime, he and his wife were still fighting a world of demons. Legal issues were still pending. Church disciplines were still in place. They were at a new church. The pastor and the council welcomed them, but they felt more like an elephant in the room than sinners saved by grace.

As weeks and months passed, depression wrapped around him like a dark cloud. He hated his new job. He hated his new life. He hated the hurt he'd caused so many people. Countless people. People who still write him in anger. He hated what he'd done to his wife. And more, what he'd done to God.

There were days he felt like he was walking down the stairs of a dungeon. Darker and darker. Colder and colder.

The smell of ancient mold filling his nostrils. The fear of eternal flames flashing in his head.

He was scared.

Except for his wife and a few straggling friends, he was alone. Very, very alone. And wondering, more than ever, if life was worth living.

It was in those days that he came home one night, bursting through the door, calling out for his wife.

"It's finished! It's done, I mean, done, over, gone!" he said. His face different. Bright. His eyes alive again.

"What are you talking about," she asked, confused.

"Today, at lunch. I had to get out of my little cubicle office space and go for a walk. There's a park nearby. I was walking, just walking. So tired of it all. And I saw this mom with her two little children. Toddlers, a boy and a girl, holding these balloons. They were all so happy until the boy let them go. And three balloons went up into the air. Higher and higher. The boy started screaming, 'Get the balloons, Mommy! Get the balloons!' She said, 'I can't. They're gone. I can't reach them anymore.' And the boy cried and cried. And quietly, in my heart, as if the Lord was standing right there, He whispered to me and said, 'Scapegoat!' Before I could wrap my mind around it, I suddenly knew what He was saying. I could see it there—in the balloons. It was over. I mean, done! Completely done!

"I couldn't get my eyes off them. I felt so sorry for the little boy. He was crying so hard. But those balloons kept getting higher and higher, smaller and smaller. The wind was taking them off to the east. And this joy, this cleansing unbelievable joy was filling my heart. I couldn't wait until I couldn't see them anymore. Smaller and smaller until, a few minutes later, they were gone! It's over, sweetheart. It doesn't matter what the courts say. It doesn't matter what people say. It's over!"

His wife had taken in his infectious joy, but she was still puzzled. "What does 'Scapegoat!' have to do with anything?"

"I'd forgotten there were two goats—not one," he thrilled. "One for sacrifice, with the high priest taking its blood into the Holy of Holies. And then the other, the scapegoat. Same story—the high priest laid his hands on it, confessed the people's sins, and then he sent it away. One great big visual. People would physically see their sins going away, getting smaller and smaller, until they couldn't see it anymore—out of sight forever.

"All this time, I've clung to Jesus being the sacrifice for my sin. In my head, I know it's true, I know I'm forgiven. But I couldn't see it. Today I saw it! I saw those balloons take off into the sky, going higher and higher, getting smaller and smaller, and I knew in my heart what I'd never known before. Jesus is also my scapegoat. He's taken my sins away 'as far as the east is from the west' (Ps. 103:12). They're gone! It's over, really over."

With that, she smiled in delight as he took her into his arms and cheered like a man who'd just won a million bucks.

The memory of that day—all these years later—is still with him. Even now, sitting in church with another wave of accusation and controversy spinning around him. He closes his eyes. He can still see the boy holding the balloons. He can still hear the sound of his screams when they left his hand, "Get the balloons, Mommy! Get the balloons!" He can still see them now.

Reaching to the skies.

And he can still hear the sound that set him free.

"Scapegoat!"

QUESTIONS FOR REFLECTION

In this broken, imperfect world, we live with people who will never forgive us for what we've done. It's part of the journey. This must not stop us from doing the work we need to do with the Lord—or with them. Will you choose it today? If not, why not?

Do you need to see balloons in your life? Do you need to visually see the scapegoat of the Bible gone into the heavens? Disappear from view? Will you ask Him for it— to see, really see?

55
POWER IN THE BLOOD

Reflections on Psalm 32:1–7

*How blessed is he whose transgression
is forgiven, whose sin is covered!*

—PSALM 32:1

Andre sat next to me in church. His Bible in one hand. A pen in the other. A notepad on his lap.

"This morning we're looking at five key steps of God's plan of forgiveness," the preacher began. "Steps that have radically changed my life."

I saw Andre out of the corner of my eye write *forgiveness* on his pad and then underline it. Of all people, I thought to myself, I'd choose him to bring the morning sermon.

Andre came from the streets. He once told me he couldn't remember a day when alcohol and drugs weren't part of his childhood. Big family. Absent father. Mom with a big heart but unable to care for her children.

He was there when the unthinkable happened.

He saw his older brother shoot and kill his mom.

I remember a day, several years back now, when he asked a group of men at our church to pray for him. He'd been sober a couple of years. He'd been in an intentional rehabilitation program. He loved to quote his lifeline Bible verse: "I can do all things through [Christ] who strengthens me" (Phil. 4:13).

"It's time," he told us, "for me to go visit my older brother in jail. I called and the date is set. I want you to pray for me. I want him to know I forgive him."

We were all dumbstruck. How does anyone do that? Forgive the man—let alone your own brother—who shot and killed your mother?

But he did just that.

"It's OK if my brother doesn't receive it," he said. "But I need to tell him. I need him to know what Jesus Christ has done for me, He can do for him. He may not get it now. But I bet he'll never forget. And maybe someday he'll believe too."

The preacher testified he'd had an abusive father. He described the impact to his self-image and how he'd spent his early adult years in reckless sin.

"The first step is to acknowledge the pain. Don't run from it. Engage the story. Know that forgiveness is a process. Sometimes a long process. The second step is to dig deep inside ourselves. We first have to forgive ourselves. If Jesus taught us to love our neighbor as we love ourselves, we have to start there. And when we're hurt, when we're beaten up, this is a hard thing to do. We need God's help. We need to learn to love ourselves again."

Out of the corner of my eye, I saw Andre writing down the steps.

"The third step is full of choices. I choose not to speak ill of the person who hurt me. I choose to pray for that person. I choose to see that person through the lens of God's love for them. I choose to take steps, as God leads, to show signs of peace toward that person. And I choose to release my pain to God."

Off on the margins of his paper, I saw Andre write in big letters, "Where is the power?" I felt like a school kid peering over at his notes.

The preacher got to the fourth step. "It's the hardest of all. We need to ask God to help us go to that person. Now for some of you this isn't possible. Maybe the person is dead. Maybe the person is too violent and you can't go back. But for many of us, we need to dig deep inside ourselves."

Again Andre wrote in big letters, "No! No! No! He doesn't get it."

The preacher went on with his story. He'd gone to his father's bedside when he was dying. Even then, he never got the blessing he needed so badly.

By this time, Andre had tuned out. It looked to me like he was writing poetry. I looked more carefully and saw something all too familiar—lyrics from the hymn "There Is Power in the Blood."

Would you be free from the burden of sin?
There's power in the blood, power in the blood;
Would you o'er evil a victory win?
There's wonderful power in the blood.
There is power, power, wonder working power

In the blood of the Lamb;
There is power, power, wonder working power
In the precious blood of the Lamb.[1]

"What are you doing?" I whispered.

"He doesn't know. He's not helping the people. He needs Jesus." He kept writing. "We don't dig deep in ourselves," Andre whispered back emphatically. "That's what counselors tell us all the time. It doesn't work. It never works. Do you think I could have forgiven my brother on my own? I couldn't do that. Nobody can. We have to go to Jesus. There's power in His blood. I'm going to tell the preacher after service," Andre said, still writing. "He's still living in the abuse of his father. He's still trying to forgive him. I've got to tell him he can't. He never can. He's got to go to Jesus for that. Not himself."

And that's exactly what he did.

I don't think I'll ever forget that Sunday morning. Andre knew more than most preachers ever know. It's rare these days to hear the message of the cross. But Andre knew. He knew the one and only key step in God's plan of forgiveness.

Run to Jesus. The power in His blood. For the forgiveness of our sin.[2]

I miss Andre. He's relapsed twice since that day. But each time, he's found his way back. I hear he's somewhere in the Midwest these days. And I hear he's clean, sober, and still singing of the "precious blood of the Lamb."

QUESTIONS FOR REFLECTION

If we treat sin lightly, we treat forgiveness lightly. It becomes something we can do on our own—with God's help. But when we know the power sin has over us, we come to the end of ourselves. Do you know what that's like? Do you need this power in the blood of Jesus?

Sometimes we can know, and teach, the principles of the Bible, but never come to experience them firsthand. For Andre, it was so real; he went to his brother in prison. Is it real for you? Real enough to act on?

NOTES

1. Lewis E. Jones, "There Is Power in the Blood," 1899, public domain, accessed June 21, 2013, http://www.cyber hymnal.org/htm/t/h/therepow.htm.

2. In Leviticus 1:4, we find the incredible word, one that fills the soul when understood, that we are *accepted*. The offering is made. The blood is shed. And we hear the words of our Father, the blessing of our Father, we are accepted!

56
ACCESS TO THE FATHER

Reflections on Acts 4:12

And there is salvation in no one else.

—Acts 4:12

"You have to read the book," a pastor told me. Turns out he's a personal friend of the author and it's on every best-seller list in the country.

I got the book and read it. It felt to me like a delightful infusion of a child's faith pouring into my veins.

This little four-year-old boy, during a life-threatening operation, caught a glimpse of heaven and slowly, over weeks and months, told his dad and mom about what he saw. His dad wrote the book. His dad's a pastor of a church.

"Daddy, what's a funeral?" the boy, Colton, asked.

"Well, buddy, a funeral happens when someone dies. A man here in town died, and his family is coming to the church to say good-bye to him."

"Did the man have Jesus in his heart?" the four-year-old asked.

"I'm not sure, Colton," his dad replied, "I didn't know him very well."

With that, Colton got worried and insisted, "He *had* to have Jesus in his heart. He *had* to know Jesus or he can't get into heaven!"

The same scene repeated at the church. It was the first time Colton had ever seen a casket. When he learned the dead man was inside, the worry came back.

"Did that man have Jesus?" Colton said, nearly shouting. "He had to! He had to!" The outburst caused his mom to snatch him up and take him outside. "He can't get into heaven if he didn't have Jesus in his heart," he kept saying.[1]

A little boy who'd spent a little time in heaven with a simple message. One that grown-ups have a hard time hearing.

At least that's been my experience.

A few weeks ago, I was at a funeral. I could tell the pastor loved the dear woman who had died. She had spent years in the church. A gentle soul, a person overflowing with kindness. That, of all her gifts, was her legacy.

The pastor's message was heartwarming as he remembered story after story of this great woman's life. He encouraged us to make godly choices and live godly lives as she had done. He wanted us to know how much God loved us. And that she was safe in heaven now. Cheering us all on.

It was a gentle, sentimental message, touching the heart. I could hear people around me responding with quiet sobs. The pastor honored the remarkable character of this woman, but in doing so forgot the simple message.

Colton's message.

Then came the eulogies. One of the woman's sons rose to the microphone. So like his mother—gracious and kind. After a few minutes of remembrance, he told us the most comforting words possible for a grieving soul. His mother knew Jesus.

"It may seem strange," he told us, "and hard to understand. But having cancer might have been the best thing that ever happened to her. Not that God caused it, but that He used it for her good [see Rom. 8:28]. It was this diagnosis, and the ominous 'less than two years to live' that moved her to turn to the Lord. We all saw her prayers answered because He changed her from being an active church-going woman to being a real and courageous follower of Jesus Christ. I am so proud of her."

There was comfort in his voice. Comfort that it was all true, what the pastor said. His mom was safe in heaven now. Because of Jesus Christ.

And then he did what Colton did. With compassion and sincerity, gentleness and care, he invited the people to have the same personal relationship with Jesus Christ. To have Him in our hearts. Now and forever.

Funny how we grown-ups avoid the subject. We get so afraid that people will think we're pushing our religion on them. But Jesus said it so clearly, "I am the way, and the truth, and the life; no one comes to the Father but through Me" (John 14:6). The message is almost too simple. The way to the Father, the way into heaven, only happens through His Son.

Because He's the only "Lamb of God who takes away the sin of the world" (John 1:29).

Because His blood is the only blood that has been presented to, and accepted by, our Father in heaven securing the forgiveness of our sins (see Matt. 26:28; Eph. 1:7; Heb. 9:11–28).

Because His death tore in two the veil that separated us from God, thereby giving us "confidence to enter the holy place by the blood of Jesus, by a new and living way which He inaugurated for us through the veil" (Heb. 10:19–20).

He is the way to the Father. The only way.

It's why the early Christians called themselves the people of the Way (see Acts 9:2; 19:9, 23; 22:4; 24:14, 22). It's why their message was a simple one.

A Colton message.

No one else. No other name.

So many people hate this about Christians. They say we're narrow-minded, intolerant of other faiths and personal beliefs, arrogant to think we're the only ones in the world who have the key to get into heaven. They find it hard to hear that a Champion has come. That He has done what no one else has ever done—or could do. He has opened the gates of eternity by His blood.

And then sent a four-year-old to tell us the good news.

QUESTIONS FOR REFLECTION

Sometimes when the news is so bad, so frightening, what we need most is simple faith, childlike faith, to see and believe in Jesus. Have you ever longed for that infusion of a child's faith and received it?

In Ephesians 2:18, we are told the best news: We have access to the Father through Christ by the Holy Spirit. *Access* is one of the most profound and beautiful words of the Bible. It can be yours today in Jesus. Can you imagine it? Are you different because of it?

NOTE

1. Todd Burpo, *Heaven Is for Real: A Little Boy's Astounding Story of His Trip to Heaven and Back* (Nashville: Thomas Nelson, 2010), 57–59.

PART 8

HOPE
IN JESUS

57

WHERE HOPE BEGINS

Reflections on Psalm 23

*Even though I walk through the valley of the shadow of
death, I fear no evil, for You are with me; Your rod
and Your staff, they comfort me.*

—PSALM 23:4

The preacher did what few do. He let us see, touch, and feel despair.[1]

It was a gorgeous day in the mountains of Colorado, he told us. Out with some of his grandchildren, playing in the vast forest near their home.

One of them, she must have been four or five, was given the task to take something back to the house to give to Grandma. And that's exactly what she did. But that's not all she did.

She decided she didn't want to stay in the house. She wanted to go back out into the woods to find her grandpa, brother, and sister. She didn't tell her grandma she was going. She didn't tell anyone. She just went.

In the woods. In the wild.

It wasn't long before Grandpa made it home. Or before he and his wife realized their little granddaughter, Brianne,

wasn't with them. That she'd gone back out. By herself.
Into a world filled with all kinds of danger. Alone.

He ran back to the woods, shouting her name.

Fifteen minutes passed. Nothing. He phoned back to the
house. Nothing. They called the police. Search and rescue
came.

An hour passed. Two hours passed. He'd gone down all
the familiar paths. Up on the rocks. Down to the stream.
He was scared she'd fallen in, that he was about to see her
little body in the water. Oh thank God, she wasn't there.
But his mind kept racing with horrifying images and
behind each one, raging, terrifying fear.

Three hours passed. Nothing.

Thousands upon thousands of acres of land. Wild animals everywhere. If night came, she'd never survive it. Not
now. It was too cold. He kept shouting her name. Shouting
until his voice went hoarse. Waiting, listening.

Just to hear that perfect little voice call back. A sound.
A cry. Anything.

Nothing. He phoned back to the house. Still nothing.

He did everything he could, taking this trail and that,
until he finally collapsed to his knees at the edge of the
stream. His hands grabbing his head, falling forward, hitting the ground, weeping. Crying out to the Lord for help.
For mercy. Pleading for the life of Brianne.

Helpless. Feeling for the first time since this beautiful
child came into the world, what life would be like without
her in it anymore. Scared, panicked way beyond anything
he'd ever known.

In the woods. In the wild.

He asked for the life of his granddaughter.

But he knew the story. He'd been a Christian and a pastor a long time. He'd been there at moments like these when the Lord answered prayers from the begging heart of a parent for their child. And he'd been there when the answer wasn't the answer they cried for in desperation. When the child died. When the lost were never found.

And he'd learned the secret. He knew it, there, on his knees, now grabbing the mud.

Here in the valley of the shadow of death where fear and evil engulf the soul, there is a rod and a staff to grab hold of and cling to with everything we've got. There is a Shepherd who never leaves. Who is everything He said He is no matter how the story goes.

Even if Brianne is never found.

Darkness and despair washed over him. He couldn't stop crying, those deep sobs from the pit of his stomach. Three and a half hours. He'd do anything to get her back. It's why he prayed the prayer most every parent knows at times like these.

Take me. Not her.

He didn't care about his career. He didn't care about the plans he and his wife had dreamed for their years of retirement. Nothing mattered. Not now. Not in comparison to his beautiful little girl.

And still he held onto the rod. The staff. The Shepherd. Knowing he had to do what he couldn't do.

Give her to Him.

Trust Him if she's found. Trust Him if she's not.

Because He is who He said He is. Always. Because He presides in this dark, terrible, broken-down, horror of a world where little girls disappear and evil somehow, mysteriously, makes us all feel terrifyingly vulnerable and helpless.

Because He is hope. The only hope. The Shepherd Himself.

In the woods. In the wild.

His cell phone rang while he knelt there. He was afraid to answer it. Too much time had passed. And plus, he'd just given her back to the Lord.

Was this it? The news he didn't want to hear?

Just the sound of his wife's voice made him get up and run. Run with everything he had inside him. Run the path home, up the mountainside and across to the opening where he could see people gathered.

And Brianne.

Where he got to do what he never thought he'd get to do again. Clutched in his arms. Lifted high in the air. Saying over and over.

I love you. I love you. I love you.

QUESTIONS FOR REFLECTION

These are the moments that test us most. Do you trust Him when the cry of your heart is heard and answered just as you'd hoped? Do you trust Him when it isn't?

Sometimes He doesn't take us out of the valley. Sometimes He has us stay. It's here where we learn that hope isn't an answer to a prayer. Hope is actually found in Him, our Shepherd. Do you know hope like this?

NOTE

1. This story has been adapted from a sermon given by preacher-performer Ken Davis, "Fully Alive" (lecture, Myrtle Beach Convention Center, Myrtle Beach, S.C., October 22, 2011), http://www.kendavis.com/personal-development/i-want-to-live/.

58

THE PROMISES OF GOD

Reflections on Psalm 103

Bless the LORD, O my soul, and forget none of His benefits;
Who pardons all your iniquities, Who heals all your diseases;
Who redeems your life from the pit, Who crowns you with
lovingkindness and compassion; Who satisfies your years with
good things, so that your youth is renewed like the eagle.

—PSALM 103:2–5

We sat in the old priest's office. I'd called him and told him the honest truth. I had a pastoral crisis on my hands far bigger than I could handle.

The story went something like this. A man had come to my office to see me. He was depressed and deeply troubled in spirit. He told me that he and his wife had been serving abroad as missionaries for four years and had come back to the States within the last six months.

"I've been to Christian counselors," he volunteered. "I've been to medical doctors. One tells me I'm suffering from exhaustion. Another tells me I need to see a psychiatrist. One person told me I'm possessed by the Devil. I don't know what to do."

He told me story after story of the suffering he and his wife endured in the developing country. From the moment they arrived, there was verbal abuse from local residents.

It soon escalated to threats. Their home was robbed more than once. All his work in translating the New Testament was seized and burned. Two years into their stay, he contracted an intestinal disease.

"I've gone through a whole battery of tests since we've been back. The doctors can't find anything wrong. Whatever it is, it's getting worse and it's painful. I can't sleep. I can't eat. I keep losing weight. It's affecting my marriage, my family, my work. Everybody says they're praying for me but nothing changes." Then he said it again, "I don't know what to do."

He looked straight at me and expected godly counsel. I knew right then that what he needed I didn't have. I could feel the despair of his heart and mind, like this huge cloud of darkness enveloping him and sucking out every ounce of hope from his soul.

He didn't say it, but I could feel it: "I can't go on like this much more."

"I want you to do something," I said, taking a chance. "I have a friend, an older priest. I want us both to go and see him. Will you do that with me?"

I saw hesitation in his eyes. And then, worse, hopelessness.

"Tell me your story," the old priest said as we sat in his office, three chairs facing each other. My friend began, just as he did with me. Occasionally, the priest asked a question and my friend did his best to reply.

"It sounds to me," the priest interjected, "that you are a Christian man."

"I am, sir." And with that my friend began to recall his early days as a Christian. His zeal for the Lord, his desire to be on the mission field. He spoke as a man who once was full of riches—and now had nothing.

I sat there wondering what this dear old priest would do now. It was clear my friend was suffering from chronic intestinal issues as well as severe depression. How does this priest help him now? What does he say or do?

With that, the priest opened his Bible and put it on his lap. He took his attention completely off my friend and his problems and began to speak of the things of the Lord. The words of Scripture began to fill the room.

The promises of God. The faithfulness and lovingkindness of God from generation to generation to those who fear Him.

"For as high as the heavens are above the earth, so great is His lovingkindness toward those who fear Him. As far as the east is from the west, so far has He removed our transgressions from us" (Ps. 103:11–12).

"For His anger is but for a moment, His favor is for a lifetime; weeping may last for the night, but a shout of joy comes in the morning" (Ps. 30:5).

The priest didn't stop. He'd read for over a half hour when I finally looked over at my friend and saw his eyes closed and tears running down his face. And then I looked at the priest, his elbows resting on the arms of the chair, his hands lifted to the Lord in quiet surrender as he kept reading.

And I saw what I hadn't seen before.

This old priest knew exactly what to do.

It was like he was climbing up the great mast of a tall sailing ship. Up and up, reading the promises of God, speaking of the kingdom of God. Up and up until he reached the crow's nest where he could see out. See ahead.

And tell my friend he was safe in the arms of the God of hope (Rom. 15:13; 1 Tim. 1:1).

With that, he stood in front of my friend and placed his hand on his forehead and anointed him in the name of the Father, the Son, and the Holy Spirit. With meticulous care, with both words and silence, he brought before the Lord all of this man's story. The insults, threats, and attacks. The loss of his work. The suffering of his body. The burden on his family. He prayed cleansing in Jesus' name.

And again he repeated the promises given by God in Scripture for moments just like these. So my friend could hear and receive them for himself. And he did. I could see it as I knelt next to both of them. This old priest had given my friend the greatest gift imaginable.

Hope in Jesus' name.

I felt right then that we were all in the presence of God. As if somehow we'd climbed the mast and jammed into the little crow's nest together, able to rise above the darkness of the present times and breathe in the fresh air of the kingdom of God.

"I felt hope again," my friend told me later. "I felt the strain and weight of these past years slowly begin to soften and melt away. As the Scriptures were read, as I remembered the Lord's promises to me, and as this man prayed for me, I felt joy again. Joy I once knew in Jesus."

He said he was still dealing with some of his physical issues. "But it's better now," he reassured me. "My hope is back, my heart is full—and I needed that more than anything else."

I will never forget that day. For the life of me, I couldn't figure out how that dear old priest would help my friend. But he did. And he helped me too. To this day, I find myself needing to climb that mast, find the crow's nest, and stay there for as long as it takes for hope to fill my soul.

And then down I go, looking, searching, until I find someone who needs it more than me.

Oh yeah, he knew exactly what to do.[1]

QUESTIONS FOR REFLECTION

There are times we simply need someone to help us fix our eyes on Jesus in the midst of the most distressing and chronic problems of life. Do you have people like this in your life? Are you able to do this for others?

This priest knew more than a formulaic reading of the promises of God. He ushered us into the presence of God and there His Word became alive and became healing to the soul. Would you ask Him for this cleansing? Would you seek Him for this hope?

NOTE

1. For further discussion, I highly recommend Iain Murray. "Pastoral Counseling," in *David Martyn Lloyd-Jones: The Fight of Faith 1939–1981* (Carlisle, Pa.: Banner of Truth, 1990), 403–423, from which this story (interwoven with my personal story) is adapted.

59

SCARLET IN THE WINDOW

Reflections on Joshua 2:8–21

When we come into the land, you tie this cord of
scarlet thread in the window through which you let us down,
and gather to yourself into the house your father and your
mother and your brothers and all your father's household.

—JOSHUA 2:18

I wasn't allowed to go see him in the hospital. And
rightly so.

We didn't know each other that well, but I considered
him a friend. Every time we met, it was like, if things we
different, we'd be best of friends. But as it was, we were
only acquaintances. Colleagues in ministry. Seeing each
other once or twice a year.

That summer, as he lay dying, I went to the hospital and
stood outside. He was on the seventh floor, west side,
fourth window from the end. I could see it. I couldn't see
him, but I pictured him there, standing close enough to the
window so I could see his face.

Looking out. Waiting. Hoping.

A year and a half earlier he was diagnosed with an
invasive cancer. The news was impossible to hear. He was
only forty-five years old. Six beautiful children ranging

from teens to elementary school. He pastored one of the largest churches in our city.

Not him. Of all people, not him.

We heard reports that the doctors caught it early. He responded well to treatment and, once over, there were about four to five months when they said he was cancer free.

But the week after Easter, it came back with a vengeance and knocked him down. A friend of mine sent me his sermon tapes from that Palm Sunday and Easter. I still have them. None of us imagined they'd be his last sermons ever preached.

Few outside his family saw him after that. He was in and out of the hospital. The doctors didn't think he'd make it through June. But he did.

And July. And August.

Looking out the window. Waiting.

She did too. Sitting on the ledge of an open window on the wall of Jericho. Her hands playing with the scarlet cord which hung over the side. Her eyes on the horizon. Waiting. Wondering.

Her life was a mess. Her body wasn't full of cancer, but her soul was. She'd given herself to a life of prostitution. She lived in an immoral, corrupt city where the only way to feed her family was to do what everything inside her screamed not to do.

Day after day. Back to the streets. Year after year. Her heart—run over, trampled down, without hope. Without God.

Save me.

She'd hidden the two Israelite spies when they came to town. She'd lied to the king to protect them. She knew their

God was the One who parted the Red Sea. He was the One who fought Israel's wars. It was Him, "the LORD, your God, He is God in heaven above and on earth beneath" (Josh. 2:11).

And soon He'd come for Jericho, she knew that, because Jericho was a wicked city full of violence, greed, and lawlessness. "The terror of you has fallen on us," she whispered to them (Josh. 2:9). "Fallen on me. Save me. Save my family."

The spies promised her they would if, and only if, she kept their mission a secret. If she gathered all her family inside the house. If she put a scarlet cord in her window. Then, and only then, would they see the cord and honor her request.

And they'd be true to their promise.

So she sits on the ledge of her window every day and waits, clutching the scarlet cord in her hand. This was it. The visible sign to the Israelites that promises were made. Vows were spoken. Though the Lord will rain down judgment on Jericho. Though the city will burn in flames. Not her. Not everyone packed into her little house on the city wall.

All because the scarlet cord hangs out her window. Oh, to feel it in her hands, hold it to her face, twirl it round and round. It makes her burst into song:

Though judgment falls all around me, it does not fall here.
For here, mercy has come to my home.
Mercy to those inside my walls.
Mercy to all those who trust the Lord![1]

Mercy. And a rush of pure hope.

For the first time, as far back as she could remember, she was filled with life. And promise. And future. And hope! Hope that she'd never return to the streets. Hope that no one would ever hurt her again. Hope that someone would keep his promise and rescue her.

Rescue her now. As she held that hope clutched tight in her hands.

Looking out the window. Waiting.

My friend died that September. And every once in a while, I go to my basement, search through old boxes, and grab his last two sermons. Every time I listen to them, I remember the day I stood outside the hospital, looking up to the seventh floor and picturing him there. Looking out. Waiting. Hoping.

A scarlet cord hung over the side.

His last Palm Sunday and Easter sermons were different in sound, in tone. He was the best of preachers. In fact, he taught seminary students how to preach. I remember him as a calm, methodical, organized man.

But not these sermons. They were full of emotion and filled with an urgency for us to see Jesus as Lord and Savior. To hear what He had done for us in His death, His resurrection, and His promise of new life to all who believe Him. Receive Him. It was as if my friend leapt out of the pulpit and gave everyone that same scarlet cord. He wanted us desperately to feel it in our hands, clutch it, twirl it, and know the power inside it—hope. Hope because it holds all the promises of God ever spoken. Grab it. Experience it. Look out the window and sing!

And that was my friend. Urging me, urging us all, to go to the ends of the earth and give everyone we meet the scarlet cord of hope and life and promise.

Just put it in the window. Clutch it tightly in your hands. Wait. Watch. And sing!

QUESTIONS FOR REFLECTION

In these stories, hope and faith meet. Both my friend and Rahab waited in hope for what had been promised. But they held in their hands something physical—a scarlet cord called faith, "the assurance of things hoped for" (Heb. 11:1). Can you feel faith inside you? Is it real to you, physical, touchable, tangible?

That scarlet cord is more than a physical object. It is an outward picture of real, tangible promises made. Like a wedding ring. Like the bread and wine at Communion. They are intended to help lift our eyes. Do they do that for you? Is there something inside you watching, waiting, singing in hope for all that is soon to come to you?

NOTE

1. There is beauty in this story that should not be missed. There is a very clear parallel between the scarlet cord outside Rahab's window and the lamb's blood on the doors of the Israelites on the first Passover night (Ex. 12:13). In both cases, the color scarlet was the sign for judgment to "pass over" these houses. And so it is today, for those protected by "the blood of the lamb" (Rev. 7:14; 12:11).

60

STRAIGHT TO THE HEART

~~~

Reflections on Psalm 34:1–8

The angel of the LORD encamps around those who
fear Him, And rescues them.

—PSALM 34:7

"Erilynne," her sister said, her voice subdued and anxious, "I'm in the emergency room."

"Kitten? What happened? Are you OK?" I could hear panic in my wife's voice. She covered the phone and whispered to me, "She hates doctors. I can't imagine her in a hospital. She must be so scared."

"Erilynne, I fell. I didn't mean to. It's my fault."

"Do you hurt anywhere?"

"My stomach hurts."

Elizabeth, or "Kitten" as Erilynne affectionately called her, was twelve years younger. She'd married in her forties, moved to the West Coast, found a church, and went into ministry with her husband. Although she suffered with mental challenges, Elizabeth was one determined lady.

She was admitted to the hospital. On the third day, after test results came back, her voice was scared. "Erilynne,

I don't want to go into surgery. But they're telling me I have to."

"Kitten, let me talk to your nurse. Can you get your nurse on the phone?"

A few minutes later we learned Elizabeth had fallen because she was anemic. Test results showed a large mass in her abdomen and the doctors had determined the best course of action was to operate immediately.

I listened as Erilynne talked and prayed with her sister. Over and over she reminded Elizabeth of how faithful the Lord had been to them down through the years. "Do you remember when . . . ?" she'd say, telling story after story.

"Yeah, I know," she said back quietly, scared.

"So listen to me, Elizabeth," Erilynne said with the tone of an older sister, "He's going to be faithful now. I promise you that."

"Yeah, I know," she said again.

It's hard to be so far away. Two sisters, one on the East Coast and one on the West. It's equally hard to run to the Scriptures, grab the promises, speak them, pray them, believe them but feel they, too, are far away.

It matters that He has spoken promises to us in His Word. But at times like these, we crave something deeper. We long to hear the Lord speak these same promises directly into our particular situation and to our anxious hearts. Saying our names. Knowing our pain, our fear, our cry. Assuring us that He hears us. And more than hears, He answers us.

This is how we prayed for Elizabeth. We asked that she'd know He was there, really there, speaking to her heart, calming her fear, and filling her with His love, real love, real hope.

"This poor man cried, and the LORD heard him and saved him out of all his troubles. The angel of the LORD encamps around those who fear Him, and rescues them" (Ps. 34:6–7).

Real hope, straight to the heart.

The operation was postponed a day. Elizabeth wanted to go home. She was worried about the people she and her husband minister to each day.

"I can't stay here. The women need me," she told her sister frankly.

Every morning, she and her husband would go to the streets looking for the homeless and hungry. Elizabeth, in particular, was burdened for homeless women. She served them, loved them, and did everything she could to provide for them. This, she knew, was the Lord's call on her life.

"Not yet, Kitten," Erilynne said gently. "But soon. You'll get to go home soon."

Her husband got to the hospital at noon that Wednesday. Elizabeth was unresponsive the day after surgery.

"Did she tell you her dream?" the woman in the next bed asked him.

"No," he said back, staring with sadness at the change in Elizabeth's face.

"Before she went into surgery, she told me she had the most beautiful dream. She said she was standing by a river. She said she heard a voice speaking to her. It was the

Father, and He said to her, 'Elizabeth,' calling her by name. 'Elizabeth, on Thursday at 5:00, I'm coming to take you home.'"

"Thursday at 5:00?" he asked, looking now at Elizabeth's roommate.

"That's what she said."

He nodded his head and knew exactly what that meant. Later that night, he went home and got everything ready. He called his pastor and church friends and told them Elizabeth was being released from the hospital the next day. He wanted to make sure everything was just right when she got home.

He was so excited. He wanted her home so badly.

The next day came, and a few minutes before 5:00, he walked into Elizabeth's hospital room surprised to see her still in bed. Still unresponsive. He grabbed her hand, looked at her face, and told her everything was ready at home. He told her he loved her. He told her everybody was asking for her and couldn't wait to see her.

He looked again and something was wrong.

Her breathing had slowed. And slowed again.

Until, at 5:00, Elizabeth took her last breath.

And there she was—standing by "a river of the water of life, clear as crystal, coming from the throne of God and of the Lamb" (Rev. 22:1). Elizabeth, her name known by her Father. His promise, spoken in a dream, given straight to her heart.

Our dear Kitten, home safe in the arms of Jesus.

QUESTIONS FOR REFLECTION

There are days we need Psalm 34 to come alive. We need the Lord's mercy to act in our story and give us what we can't find here in this world—real hope. Will you ask Him for this? Will you help others ask Him for this?

There is an intimacy about this story that is hard to sometimes take in. Our Father knows us by name. He knows our times. He knows our every need. And He knows how to meet us in the scariest of times. Do you turn to or run from this kind of intimacy? Do you keep it as knowledge in your head, or do you let it soak down deep in your heart?

61

HOPE HAS A NAME

~~~

Reflections on Job 19:23–29

*As for me, I know that my Redeemer lives, and at
the last He will take His stand on the earth.*

—JOB 19:25

I've often wished I was a different kind of preacher.
I admire those who have the gift of teaching, expositing
the Scriptures in a clear, controlled manner. Even when I
try, I find myself failing miserably. I always seem to get
caught at the crossroads where the great truths of the Bible
intersect with me, our times, our struggles, our hardships,
our pains.

The crossroads, where Bible and life meet.

A few years ago, I was speaking at a church on Ruth
1:16–17 where this noble woman of God, Ruth the Moabitess,
binds herself in a legal vow of undying faithfulness and
loyalty to her mother-in-law, Naomi. This is nothing less
than a picture of the same bond of covenant the Lord has
made between us and Him.

And Him and us. And us between each other. Bonds we
keep breaking and breaking.

That morning just before I stepped into the pulpit, the senior pastor announced that two of their leaders were at odds and were in a broken, unreconciled relationship, forcing one of them to leave the church. He called everyone to urgent prayer for them and to beg God's mercy for this situation. The grief that fell on the congregation was palpable.

And there I stood, in the pulpit, at the crossroads.

One moment with Ruth, the foreigner, who portrayed the kind of stubborn, unrelenting steadfast love that only comes from God—love that doesn't break. Love that sticks and sticks and refuses to break no matter what. The next moment, I was there with these people who were reeling in shock, hurt, and confusion for the break between two of their beloved leaders.

I couldn't help it. I hate when it happens. But I found, as I pleaded for the duty and responsibility of all Christians to stubbornly fight, and fight again, for the relationships given us in Christ and by Christ, my voice cracked. Tears came and I wept.

It's at times like these, I feel the tiniest glimpse of God's heart breaking as the bonds between us—for whom He died—keep breaking. And breaking. And breaking.

And then I saw a most extraordinary sight. This young man coming toward me.

Straight down the aisle of the church. A young man with Down's Syndrome, his face as bright as an angel, walking toward me with tissues in his hands.

"Why are you sad?" he asked me in a whisper. And then he reached out his arms, put them around my waist and hugged me. Hugged me and hugged me, tight and tighter still.

In front of everybody. Refusing to let go.

What we make so complicated, he made so simple.

In my prayers, I've replayed that scene over and over. At first, I didn't know why this young man was coming down the aisle. Was he going to his seat, or did he have something else in mind? Was he going to disrupt the service? But the closer he got, the more I saw. The more I realized he was coming for me. I saw the gentleness, the concern in his face. The tissues in his hand.

And I find myself wanting him to keep coming.

I saw what I think Job saw. In the midst of his greatest suffering, as he struggled to figure out why the Lord allowed him to go through such devastating loss, such personal pain, he suddenly felt this burst of hope. Hope in the promises of God. Hope in what He will do in days to come. But more. Much more.

He knew that hope is found in a Person. Hope has a name.

It's as if the Lord gave him the gift to lift his eyes and see Him coming straight down the corridor of time with gentleness and concern in His face.

Straight down the aisle with tissues in His hand.

"As for me, I know that my Redeemer lives, and at the last He will take His stand on the earth. Even after my skin is destroyed, yet from my flesh I shall see God; whom I myself shall behold, and whom my eyes will see and not another. My heart faints within me!" (Job 19:25–27).

And I find myself wanting Him to keep coming.

"Let me tell you about that young man," a dear friend said to me after the service. "He's such a godsend. One

Sunday morning, some of the children put on a play for the church. It was a modern version of the parable of the good Samaritan. A child was riding her bike and had a nasty fall. Another child came walking by, saw the young girl hurt by the fall, and passed right on by without helping. I bet you can guess what happened next," she went on, smiling.

"Well, that young man was sitting in the audience. The moment he saw her fall, he got up from his seat, came running down the aisle, got on stage, and helped her back on the bike! Of course, the children were upset because he ruined their play. So they started it all over again. And when that little girl fell a second time, the same thing happened. That big-hearted young man came running down the aisle and helped her back on the bike. But this time, as soon as he saw she was OK, he said in a rather loud but kind voice, 'You've got to stop falling now.' It was just so beautiful and everybody loved it. Well, except the kids."

As she told the story, I felt that young man's hug again. A hug that refused to let go. A hug that doesn't let our relationships break. A hug that makes sure the fallen are picked up, dusted off, and made well again. A hug with a handful of tissues.

When will our breaking stop? When will we be like Him and refuse to let go? When will we make what we make so complicated simple again?

I want to see what Job saw. I want to feel that burst of hope in my soul. Hope in His promises. Hope in our weeping. Hope that squeezes tightly and whispers His name.

And I find myself wanting Him to keep coming.

QUESTIONS FOR REFLECTION

How can we find real identity in Christ if we refuse to love each other as He has loved us? There are too many broken relationships in our church families and in the lives of our leaders. Where is the impulse to get up, run down aisles, and make a difference?

So often we don't know what to say or do when relationships break, when people suffer as Job did. But Job tells us about the gift he got—eyes to see his Redeemer, his hope. We need that gift. Will you ask Him for it? And if you have it, will you help others receive it?

62

IF WE COULD CHANGE THE PAST

Reflections on Luke 24:25–27

*O foolish men and slow of heart to believe in all
that the prophets have spoken!*

—LUKE 24:25

We sat on the stairs going down to the beach. It was a late afternoon in mid-October and except for a few stray walkers, the beach was empty.

"I wish I could take it all back," he sighed.

"You surprise me," I said, half in jest. "You're the talk of the town." And he was. In church a few Sundays back, he shared his dramatic story.

"I have to tell you," he testified that day, "I was scared. As I lay on that gurney, waiting for emergency heart surgery, feeling the weight of a New York Giants' linebacker sitting on my chest, I overheard two doctors say they weren't sure whether I'd make it or not. If that doesn't make you pray to God, I don't know what will," he bantered with the congregation. "I was begging Him for my life. I didn't want to die. I didn't want to leave my family. I wasn't ready and I needed help.

"A few minutes later, just before they put me under anesthesia, I heard the Lord say to me, 'Why don't you believe in Me?' At first, I didn't understand. 'No!' I said quickly, 'You know I believe in You.' In my head, I mounted my defense. I've been at the church fifteen years. I'm an elder. I've spoken at dozens of church conferences. 'Lord,' I prayed again, 'don't You know? . . .'

"Then a second time, He said, 'Why do you refuse to repent of your sin?' As I heard these words, my brilliant defense turned to ash. I could see my heart—my real heart. I saw it, and when I saw it, I knew what I've known all along.

"I am two people. I am a corporate businessman. It's been my life for thirty years. I put on that suit, I head to the train, and I become a man governed by the principles that govern the kingdom of this world. And I do it well. Always have.

"But when I get home and take off that suit, I change into being a husband, a dad, a Christian man, an elder of this church. I'm the guy around here people turn to when wise counsel is needed in business. I'm the guy some men look up to because I'm successful, I'm rich, and I confess Christ for my life.

"Two people, that's what I am. Two very different people. Just as I put on the image of the corporate businessman during the week, so I put on the image of being a Christian here at church. And worse, I've known it all along.

"But laying there on that gurney? I wasn't either man. I was me.

"I remember when I first came to this church, the Lord was working on me. Nearly every service He showed me the sins of my past. He let me see the real me, a sinner in His sight. And I'd get on my knees, humble myself before the Lord, and repent of my sin. But it's not what you think. An awful, evil thought snuck into my mind. I was suddenly aware if I did get on my knees, people would see. I'd gain respect in the church. I'd be a legitimate follower of Christ. In time, I could be a leader in this church and make a name for myself here.

"That was fifteen years ago. All this time, I've been able to fool you. Fool my family. Even fool myself. But laying on that gurney, literally scared to death, scared *of* death, I knew I hadn't fooled God.

"There was only one heart surgery that really mattered that day. I needed to get right with the Lord. I needed to come face-to-face with my sin, arrogance, and pride. I needed to confess and repent from serving the gods of success, power, and fame both in the corporate world and here in the church.

"And I did. I asked Him to forgive me in Jesus' name. I told Him I was sorry, and I thanked Him and thanked Him again that He loved me enough to give me another chance.

"And this morning, I am here to ask for your forgiveness too."

"What do you mean you wish you could take it all back?" I asked as we sat there, looking over the ocean.

"I've wasted so many years. If I'd given my life to Christ fifteen years ago, I mean, really surrendered my life and lived it for Him and not for me, I'd be a different man today. Our kids would be different. I'd have made wildly different decisions. My wife and I could have been part of building His kingdom, not mine. But no," he said sharply, looking straight at me, "Jesus said it in Luke 24:25: 'O foolish men and slow of heart to believe in all that the prophets have spoken!' He's talking straight talk right to me. I've read the Prophets. I've read the Gospels. I know my Bible. But I didn't know Him. And I didn't live for Him," he said, putting his hands over his face.

We sat there for a while in silence, listening to the waves crash on shore.

I wondered then what it would be like to grant his wish. To turn back time and live the years again knowing what we know now. To do it all over again but this time with a new heart. If we just believed . . . if we could change the past and rewrite the story of our lives.

Then go back further. How different it all would have been had we believed what the prophets had said. We would have been ready. Ready for His birth. Ready to welcome Him. We'd have invited the entire world to come the moment the star appeared. We'd have been there, together, to celebrate the birth of the King of all kings, our Emmanuel. There would have been song! There would have been dancing! All the world would have bowed their knee that night in Bethlehem.

If we could rewrite the story.

If we had just believed.

QUESTIONS FOR REFLECTION

We sometimes do image so well we actually believe it's our real identity. Then moments like these come when the light of the Holy Spirit hits our hearts and we see the difference between image and real identity in Jesus. Can you see the difference in your life?

If you could rewrite your story—this time, believing—what would be different?

63
UNDISTRACTED EYES

Reflections on Luke 2:25–38

*She never left the temple, serving night and
day with fastings and prayers.*

—LUKE 2:37

For thirty years, we've had male Old English Sheepdogs. These dogs were born to herd. Give them sheep—or really, anything that breathes—and they'll circle, gather, and lead with one eye on the sheep and one eye on the shepherd.

Through the years I've trained our "boys" to go off leash. So when it's just the two of us out for a walk, they'll go off to smell the land, chase a stray squirrel, or take off on a run. And every once in a while, I'll find that split second they're not looking and dart behind a tree.

I remember Barnabas most of all. He was our last boy. Within seconds, he'd see I was gone. I'd watch his body freeze as I would peek out from behind the tree. He was waiting for movement. Sound. Smell. Nothing. And he'd realize.

I was gone.

He'd bolt to the last place he saw me. Not far from the tree. Again, he'd freeze. His body rigid, his motions jerky, his head to the right, then the left, with just enough hair in his eyes not to see me.

Then he'd take off—fast—to where I could have gone, should have gone. And again he'd freeze. But this time I think I'd see panic in him—or is it in me?—that maybe, just maybe, he'd really lost me. Lost me for good. A squirrel moves on the grass thirty yards away. A car passes on the street. Barnabas sees none of it. Finding me, that's all that matters to him now.

I can't play this game long. I don't know why I play it at all. It somehow brings back nightmares from my childhood. Nightmares when suddenly Mom and Dad were gone—I mean, really gone. I'd run everywhere to find them, but I couldn't and I'd start screaming. Screaming loud enough to wake myself up.

I know that panic.

And I'd sit up in bed, my eyes fixed on the door, waiting, hoping that soon they'd come for me. Soon it would be all over and I'd find them. They'd find me.

And I can't stand it any longer. It makes me come out from behind the tree.

When I think of the Old Testament saints who died waiting for all that God promised them, I think most of Simeon and Anna. They knew it. They got it. They understood by revelation of the Holy Spirit that all the promises of God found their fulfillment in the coming of "the Lord's Christ" (Luke 2:26). The world spun around them in chaos and confusion, but none of that mattered.

One thing mattered.

They were looking for Him. Looking for their Comforter, their Savior, a light to the Gentiles, the glory of Israel, the Redeemer of their people (see Luke 2:25, 30, 32, 38). For this reason, Simeon stayed near the temple, and Anna never left it.

She prayed; she fasted. She served the Lord night and day as a young widow. As a middle-aged woman. Right up to the age of eighty-four. Never slowing, never stopping the search. And I picture her with that same intensity, same zeal, same panic deep inside her as I remember in the eyes of my boy Barnabas. As I remember as a child.

She was looking for Him. She was waiting, hoping, longing with expectation, as if at any moment she's going to see Him. He's going to come. She's going to find Him and she's going to be found by Him. And the miracle of Anna's story is that she's not like all the Old Testament saints who went before her. All of them died in faith, holding in their hearts the hope of Him who was to come (Heb. 11:13, 39–40).

She's different. Different because she lived to hear the unimaginable. The sound of a baby's cry. And not just any baby. The Bible lets us see her standing next to Simeon as he holds the Child, saying what every saint in every generation before them wanted to say, "For my eyes have seen Your salvation" (Luke 2:30).

Then we get to see Anna—the last time we see her—speaking of Jesus "to all those who were looking for" Him (Luke 2:38). And I want what she had.

But I realize I've been like my boy Barnabas. Time and time again, I've been distracted by the world around me and I've taken my eyes off the Shepherd. But today I want that passion of Simeon and Anna—that hope, that panic, back deep in my soul—to long for the day of His coming. That day when we shall see Him face-to-face (1 John 3:2; Rev. 22:4).

And be found.

There was nothing like the joy I saw in Barnabas's face as I came out from behind the tree and called his name. He'd come running at me so excited and at full blast. I mean, scary full blast, because this hairy Old English Sheepdog wouldn't slow down as he got closer. And then, boom! He'd knock me to the ground, wagging his whole body and licking me silly.

And I get it. I really get it. Because I knew what it was like when I'd wake up in that bed at night so scared and then hear the sound of my mom and dad coming down the hall, flipping on the lights, and taking me into their arms.

That feeling of being safe again.

I miss Barnabas. After thirty years of male Old English Sheepdogs, we now have our first little girl. Her name is L'Oreal, named after the cosmetic company whose byline is "Because you're worth it." And she is, she knows it, and she plays her supermodel role to the hilt!

Every once in a while on our walks together, I'll get that itch to sneak behind a tree when she's not looking. Then I'll peek around to watch her and, to my surprise, my little Old English Sheepdog diva girl doesn't even notice I'm gone. Because she, like me, is too caught up in her own little world.

QUESTIONS FOR REFLECTION

Have you ever felt that same panic deep in your soul?

One eye on the Shepherd and everything that spins in chaos in our lives comes to order. Is that true for you? Do you live with one eye on the Shepherd? Or do you live distracted?

64

NIGHT TRAVELERS

Reflections on Matthew 2:1–12

Now after Jesus was born in Bethlehem of Judea in the days
of Herod the king, magi from the east arrived in Jerusalem,
saying, "Where is He who has been born King of the Jews?
For we saw His star in the east and have come to worship Him."

—MATTHEW 2:1–2

I sat at the far end of the first row for the annual Christmas play. The children were adorable in their costumes, most a little shy to be on stage, especially with their parents constantly waving and filming their every move.

I had no idea this little play was about to impact my life.

The play went like this—a young reporter was interviewing the three magi shortly after they'd seen the Child. He wanted to know why they seemed so troubled.

"We saw His star," one said, "and we were filled with joy. We knew this was a sign from God above. A diviner like us, a magi from centuries back, spoke by the Spirit of God. He told the world that this star would appear in Israel announcing the birth of a great King. And now that day has come!"

"We went back and read," another said, "and reread the ancient records of the Jews. It's all there. The coming of their Messiah, the son of David, whom the prophets of old said was more than a great King. They said He was Emmanuel, both the King who is God and the God who is to be born."

"When we saw His star, we knew we had to go see Him," the third one said. And then they began to talk, one right after the other, blending their voices as one.

"But would they let us? We didn't know. We told our families. We told our government officials. We brought the finest, most expensive gifts possible. We could only hope the Jewish leaders would allow us an audience with the King, so we too might see Him and worship Him."

The reporter kept watching as the three men talked to him. He tried to catch what they were saying, but it left him puzzled and strangely speechless.

"We imagined all Israel would be in Jerusalem like they do at their feasts. Everyone celebrating with song and dance, food and drink, cheering at the sight of the royal Child and rejoicing with the greatest joy that His reign and His kingdom were here—finally here!"

"Then we realized we were thinking too small," one magi said.

"Maybe the whole world saw the star like we did and were doing just what we were doing. We actually believed that Jerusalem, no, all of Israel, wouldn't be able to contain the amount of people coming from foreign lands to worship the Child."

And with that, disappointment fell on their faces. The reporter picked up on it and asked why.

"Because that's not the story. We got to Jerusalem and it was no different than any other day. We went up to the religious officials and asked, 'Where is He who has been born King of the Jews?' In no time, we were summoned to see King Herod. We told him about the star and that we'd come to worship the newborn King. And we could see that deeply troubled him."

"It was like he never heard it before. He knew about the star. He knew about the coming of the Messiah. He knew the ancient prophecies. But no one had made the connection. Not him. Not the Jewish leaders. Suddenly all of Jerusalem knew that we'd come—and why we'd come—and were as troubled as Herod," one magi said.

"But still, even then, they didn't get it. They didn't understand," another added.

"King Herod sent us secretly to Bethlehem where the prophets said Messiah, son of David, the great Emmanuel King was to be born."

"We thought for sure all of Jerusalem would make the trek with us from Jerusalem to Bethlehem, following the star, in hope to see their Messiah."

"But no one came with us. So we thought, surely the people of Bethlehem had seen the star and knew about the birth of the Child. Surely this great town would be filled to the brim with people and joyous celebration. But it wasn't. We couldn't believe it. This is the city of David. This is where the prophets said He'd be born. We asked people in town but no one seemed to know anything about why the star had appeared, what it meant, or that it shouted the news—the promised Son of David had just been born to them! They didn't know or even seem to care."

"So we kept on following the star until it led us to the place where the royal family stayed. We knocked and someone greeted us. The moment the door of that old barn opened, we saw the Child and instantly fell to the ground and worshiped Him."

"The Lord had prospered our way."

"He gave us audience into His royal presence."

"But it was just us and no one else. We were told about the shepherds on the night of His birth and what the angels had said. We were told stories of how the angel Gabriel had visited His mother Mary and how God visited Joseph in a dream. We knew all the Scriptures God had spoken were true."

"But it was just us and no one else," one said, sadly.

"The people—they all saw the star. They all knew the Scriptures. But no one could put the two together. They went on with their busy lives not knowing that the greatest moment of all time had come upon them as foretold in God's holy Word and announced by the sending of the King's star. And even when we told them, they showed no interest. They weren't moved by it."

"They weren't ready. No one was!"

"There were no crowds around the Child. No songs or cheers or dances. No streets filled with food and drink, entertainment and joy. No central platforms built so that all the people could see Him, honor Him, and worship Him."

"We thought the whole world was going to be here with us. We never dreamed that we'd be one of the only ones who'd get an audience with the great King."

"Why weren't they ready? Why was there no one here to welcome Him?"

And with that, the children bowed.

My busy, little world suddenly stood still. I knew then that times had not changed. That I was no different than the people of that day.

The Scriptures in one hand. Life in the other. And the two rarely meeting. And I wondered what I'm missing today. Missing because I'm too busy. Too busy to follow the night travelers on their quest. To find Jesus. To worship Jesus. And to follow Him with all my heart, soul, mind, and strength.

QUESTION FOR REFLECTION

When God's Spirit is united to our hearts and minds, how can the Scriptures remain in one hand and life in the other?